THIRD EDITION

THE ILLUSTRATED GUIDE TO THE

AMERICAN

ECONOMY

BY HERBERT STEIN & MURRAY FOSS
WITH THE ASSISTANCE OF MATTHEW CLEMENT

THE AEI PRESS

Publisher for the American Enterprise Institute

Washington, D.C.

1999

Available in the United States from the AEI Press, c/o Publisher Resources Inc., 1224 Heil Quaker Blvd., P.O. Box 7001, La Vergne, TN 37086-7001. Distributed outside the United States by arrangement with Eurospan, 3 Henrietta Street, London WC2E 8LU England.

Library of Congress Cataloging-in-Publication Data
    The illustrated guide to the American economy / by Herbert Stein & Murray Foss.
    p. cm.
    Includes bibliographical references (p.).
    ISBN 0-8447-4104-3 (pa.: alk. paper). –ISBN 0-8447-4103-5 (cl.: alk. paper)
    1. United States–Economic conditions–1981– I. Stein, Herbert, 1916–.
II. Foss, Murray F. III. Title.
HC106.8.S7414 1999
330.973'092–dc21

                                                                99-39716
                                                                CIP

The AEI Press
Publisher for the American Enterprise Institute
1150 17th Street, N.W., Washington, D.C. 20036

Printed in the United States of America

To B. G.
and A. F.

Contents

Part One: A Rich Country

Part Two: Uses of the National Output

Part Three: Who Produces the National Output?

Part Four: Distribution of the National Income

Part Seven: Personal Incomes

Part Eight: Distribution of Income

Part Thirteen: Government Expenditures, Taxes, and Deficits

Part Fourteen: Health

Preface to *The Illustrated Guide,* Third Edition

We produced *The Illustrated Guide to the American Economy* in 1992 and its second edition in 1995 in the belief that talk about the American economy suffered from a lack of information and that an attempt to present some basic facts would be helpful. The response to the two previous editions prompts us to believe that a revised and updated edition would be valuable. It comes at a time when interest in economic statistics is greater than ever before. There has been an acceleration in the pace of economic research, from which new facts have emerged, and basic statistics have been revised in ways that affect not only ongoing developments but also, to some extent, our view of history.

We have added new material since the first edition. One section (part fourteen) extends the discussion of health issues; the policy debate in the early 1990s highlighted the importance of this section. Another (part fifteen) takes up the shortcomings of our price indexes and problems in measuring changes in the quality of life, including environmental issues. This part embraces some criticisms of the consumer price index in the report of the Advisory Commission to Study the Consumer Price Index (the Boskin report), as well as new initiatives in price measurement by the Bureau of Labor Statistics. The discussion of capital in part five has been broadened to include government capital and infrastructure, natural resources, and research and development. Although education is not treated as capital here, there is more discussion of the role of education in the working of the labor market. Part five now contains a fuller treatment of saving than before.

The section concerning the structure of the economy (part ten) now discusses small business, multinational corporations, and trade unions. It also takes up the changing structure of banking and public utilities that followed the spread of deregulation and new technology. Part eleven, on wealth and debt, pays greater attention to the stock market, mutual funds and pension funds, and how household balance sheets have been affected by the boom in equities. Material dealing with the distribution of income in the United States has been expanded (part four). Part eight, on the distribution of income, and part nine, on poverty, now give more recognition to alternatives to the conventional measurements.

This new edition brings the data up to or through the year 1998, when that is possible, in addition to incorporating other changes. One of those is to follow the practice of the Bureau of Economic Analysis of the U.S. Department of Commerce in shifting from the gross national product (GNP) to the gross domestic product (GDP) as the basic measure of national output. Of greater importance are the 1996 revisions instituted by BEA; as a result of these, changes in real output and in prices are being measured much more accurately today than in the past.

A note to the volume on page 280 contains a brief treatment of some technical problems.

We owe a large debt to Matthew Clement for his excellent research assistance and computer skills. We wish also to thank Virginia Bryant, Kenneth Krattenmaker, James Morris, Jean-Marie Navetta, Ann Petty, and Jennifer Smith, who have assisted in the production of the present volume.

This book, like the two previous editions, was a joint effort by Herbert Stein and Murray Foss. Herbert Stein died on September 8, 1999, shortly before the book went to press.

From the Introduction to the First Edition

Presidents, cabinet members, congressmen, senators, TV pundits, editorial writers, leaders of business and labor, and taxpayers talk about the American economy. That is natural and good. Much of our lives centers on the economy. A great deal of this talk, though, proceeds in ignorance of basic facts about the American economy or, what is worse, makes assumptions about it that are not so—or at least are highly doubtful.

Listening to TV or reading the newspapers raises a long list of questions whose answers would be relevant to the national discussion but are commonly unknown, ignored, or misunderstood, such as:

- How rich is the American economy, compared with other times and other countries?
- How is the national income divided—between profits and labor compensation, for example—and what are the recent trends in that division?
- What do the American people spend their money on?
- Is America becoming a "service economy"?
- How serious have recessions been?
- What is happening to the relative earnings of women or blacks compared with white males?
- What is the extent of poverty in America?
- How heavy are American tax burdens today compared with earlier times and other countries?
- What have been the effects of budget deficits?
- What caused the large increase of the U.S. trade deficit?

This book was written in the belief that a certain number of basic facts about the economy, important to the continuing discussion, could be identified and presented in a readily understandable way. By "basic" facts we mean those that refer to the condition of the country as a whole, that affect and interest large numbers of people, and that throw some light on the subjects of most widespread concern.

The word fact is more difficult to define. What we mean by fact in this book is what can be measured, expressed in numbers, and presented in charts. We recognize that much about the American economy cannot be described in this way. After all, as Adam Smith said, the economy is governed by an "invisible hand," and if it is invisible, we cannot make a chart of it. The facts we present are the outcome of the behavior of hundreds of millions of individuals. To describe and explain the behavior of these individuals and the interactions among them is the subject matter of economics, political science, psychology, and other disciplines beyond the purview of this book, or of any other except in quite abstract terms. Other important aspects of the economy—freedom, variety, justice, the quality of life—can be presented here only marginally, if at all.

Still, the kinds of facts we present here are important: they say much about the conditions we live with and constantly discuss.

Measurement of economic conditions and changes is inherently difficult for many reasons. What we are interested in is real conditions and changes that affect real people, but we have no way of acquiring all the information we would want about all the people and no totally satisfactory way of adding it all up if we could get it.

The problem of measurement may be illustrated by reference to one of the most common pieces of economic information, the consumer price index (CPI). Consumers buy millions of different products (including services) in different places in the country and in different stores. So consumers pay millions of different prices. No one can collect all these prices. In fact, the CPI is based on a carefully drawn sample of all prices, running into the hundreds of thousands but certainly not including all prices. Then we face the problem of adding all these prices together to get a single number of the month or year that can be compared with a single number for another month or year. We cannot simply say that every price counts equally—the price of an automobile to be added to the price of a (pound, ton?) of spinach. So we give each price a weight in proportion to how much "consumers" spend on the product.

But different consumers spend different amounts on different products. If the price of spinach goes up, that is not an increase in consumer prices for someone who hates spinach and never buys it. We are necessarily forced to rely on averages that may not fit one person very well. We also have a big problem in defining the "product" that is being priced. Products change in quality from one time to another, and it is hard to tell how much of the change in the price reflects a change in the price for the real value provided or a change in the real value provided.

Such difficulties bedevil much of the information we present here. But the statistical agencies that produce the data we use devote many resources and much talent to deal with these hazards as well as they can. Whatever their limitations, the results are superior to the casual and random observations that we would otherwise often have to rely on in thinking about the economy. But these inevitable difficulties are a warning against placing much weight on small and brief variations in the data. If the statistics show that the CPI rose at 10 percent a year during one decade and 5 percent in another we may rather confidently say that there was more inflation in one case than in the other. One could not be sure about the significance of a statistic showing 5 percent in one year and 6 percent in another.

In the pages that follow we have tried to confine the presentation to data of significant magnitude and durability. We have not made much of minutiae, and we have not made forecasts.

The selection and presentation of information here are as objective as we can make them. We have tried not to make a book of Republican or Democratic, conservative or liberal, optimistic or pessimistic data, and as we look at what has emerged we do not think the result is biased. We believe that most would agree that any reasonable description of the American economy would have to include much of the information we present here. Moreover, we have not sought exotic or iconoclastic data. We have not looked for things that would surprise the reader, although, despite the fact that both of us have spent about fifty years with statistics like these, some things did surprise us.

Most of the information presented here relates to the period since 1947. Not going back earlier was dictated partly by the availability of data but mainly by the belief that the Great Depression and World War II were a watershed, before which relevance falls off rapidly. In some cases, however, information is carried back to 1929 and in a few cases earlier than that.

The data used herein came, of course, from a large variety of sources to which we are totally indebted. None of the people who helped us is responsible for errors the book may contain. For each of the subjects covered here one or the other of us was primarily responsible for selecting the data, designing the chats, and writing the text, but we have joint responsibility for the final product.

(1992)

THIRD EDITION

THE ILLUSTRATED GUIDE TO THE

AMERICAN ECONOMY

PART ONE

A Rich Country

Total output in the United States has increased greatly from generation to generation.

Total output and output per capita are the best available single measures of the performance of an economy. The total output of a country limits how much its inhabitants can consume, how much they can devote to investment to increase consumption, and how much they can devote to the defense of the country.

We must immediately emphasize that estimates of total output cannot be precise and that estimates of change over long periods are necessarily only crude approximations. For one thing, national output consists of millions of different goods and services; we have no completely satisfactory way of converting them to a common unit so that they can be added together. In practice, different products are added together in proportion to their relative prices. But these relative prices change over time, and the measured path of output depends on the year of the prices used.

In the accompanying charts, output before 1929 is based on estimates of real output that used 1929 price weights. Output figures since 1929, however, are Bureau of Economic Analysis (BEA) data that reflect the use of chained quantity indexes in which price weights were changed each year. All the data in the charts on page 5 are expressed as indexes with 1929 equal to 100. Output is measured by the gross domestic product (GDP). GDP is the sum of the total output of goods and services produced within the borders of the United States. It does not precisely equal the output owned by Americans, which is the gross national product (GNP), because some output produced within our borders belongs to foreigners and Americans own some output produced abroad. For the United States, the difference between GDP and GNP is tiny, although that is not true for all countries.

With a few exceptions, GDP as measured includes only output that is bought or sold in markets. Thus, GDP leaves out some important items—notably, unpaid work performed within the household. In addition, good data may not exist even for the things that are included.

While no great weight should be placed on the calculation that per capita GDP in 1999 was almost ten times as high as in 1889, all reported direct observations of life in America confirm that there has been a great increase in per capita output in that period.

We must be cautious about interpreting the increase in output per capita as evidence of a similar increase in "well-being" or "happiness." Whether people are better off with the higher output and incomes depends on what they do with them.

TOTAL REAL GROSS DOMESTIC PRODUCT OF THE UNITED STATES, 1889–1998

INDEX: 1929=100

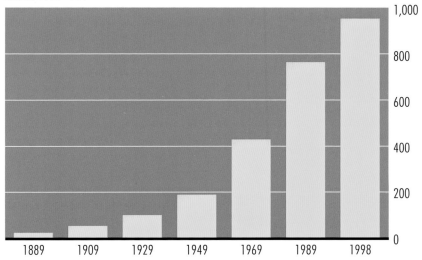

REAL GROSS DOMESTIC PRODUCT PER CAPITA OF THE UNITED STATES, 1889–1998

INDEX: 1929=100

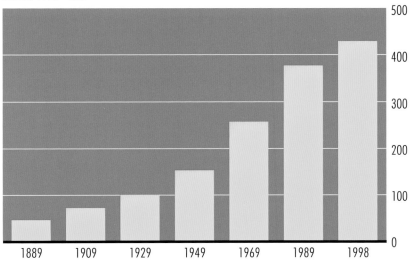

Note: The first five bars are spaced twenty years apart, but there are only nine years between the last two bars.

Total output per capita is significantly higher in the United States than in other large "rich" countries— one-fourth higher than in Japan.

A precise comparison of total output in different countries is as difficult as a precise comparison of output in widely separated years in the same country. We know the value of the output of each country in its own currency, but we have no precise, accurate way of converting those values into a common currency. In 1997, for example, the Japanese GDP was 507 trillion yen, whereas the U.S. GDP was $8.0 trillion. But how many yen are equal to a dollar in terms of the amount of goods and services that they represent? We cannot answer that question with certitude because the mixture of products in the two economies differs and because the relative prices of the same products in the two countries differ. The best, though imperfect, way to arrive at an answer involves two steps. First, the cost in yen and in dollars of the American mixture of goods and services is calculated to get one measure of the relative value of the yen and the dollar. Then, the same calculation is made for the Japanese mixture to get another measure of the relative value of the two currencies. An average of the two resulting yen/dollar ratios is used to translate the Japanese GDP from yen into dollars.

The chart shown here is based on such calculations. Common, but much less reliable, calculations are based on the market exchange rates of different currencies. Those sometimes show per capita GDP higher in Japan or in Germany than in the United States. The market exchange rates, however, do not reflect the purchasing power of the currencies for the full range of goods and services included in a country's total output. Moreover, the exchange rates vary greatly from year to year; calculations based on those rates bear no relation to the changes in real output.

GROSS DOMESTIC PRODUCT PER CAPITA FOR SELECTED COUNTRIES, 1998

AS A PERCENTAGE OF U.S. PER CAPITA GDP

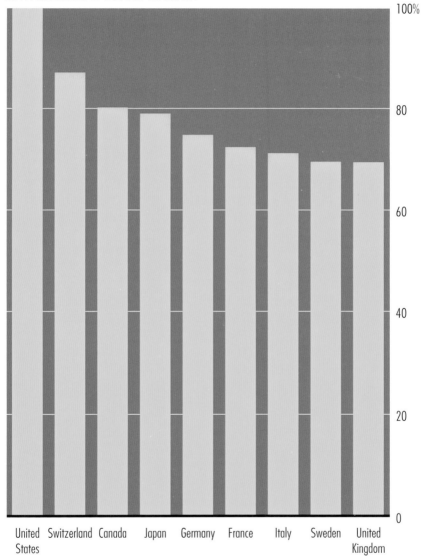

In this century, all countries that we now call *advanced* have grown at rates that are quite exceptional by comparison with longer periods of history.

During the twentieth century, per capita output in the United States and in other advanced countries has increased by about 1–2 percent per year. In a few periods in a few countries in the most distant past, per capita output may have grown as rapidly. For most of human history, though, the rates of growth must have been much lower, and there were some periods of decline.

One might suppose that, in the first year of the Christian era, per capita income in the most advanced place, presumably Rome, was about $1,000 a year, equal to that in Bangladesh today. If per capita output had increased from that level to the level in the United States today, about $20,000, that would have been an annual rate of increase of about 15/100 of 1 percent, compared with an annual rate of increase of 1.8 percent experienced in the United States in this century. That is to say, we and others in the industrial countries have been living in a period of unusually rapid economic growth.

As the chart shows, the growth rate was lower during this century in the United States than in the other countries shown—except for the United Kingdom. Per capita output is higher in the United States today, because it was already higher in 1900 than in the other countries—again excepting the United Kingdom. In 1900, the per capita output of Japan, for example, was less than 30 percent of that of the United States.

GROWTH OF OUTPUT PER CAPITA, 1900–1997

ANNUAL RATE

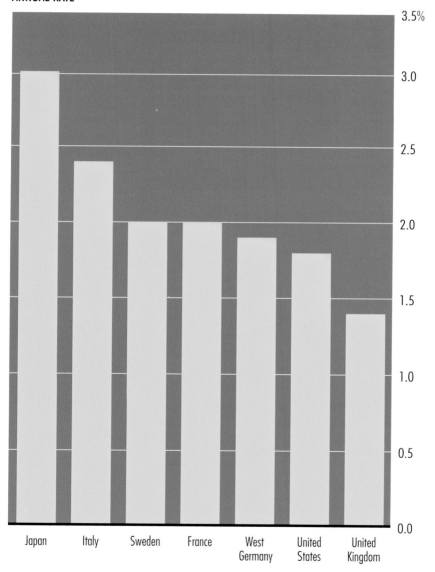

Most of the world's population lives in countries where output per capita is far below that of the United States, but the gap has been narrowing for some of the largest countries.

In 1996, more than 70 percent of the world's population lived in countries with a per capita gross domestic product less than 20 percent of that of the United States. This calculation is based on estimates of the World Bank, which attempts to measure and compare the real purchasing power of the currencies of the various countries. Of course, the difficulties already noted about making international comparisons of total or per capita output are especially severe when countries as different as the United States and Bangladesh are involved. If these calculations imply that a person in Bangladesh has an income equivalent to less than $3 a day, they do not mean that a person in Bangladesh lives as a person with an income of only $3 a day would live in the United States. But there is no doubt that the differences in per capita income are very large.

The concentration of population in the group with less than 20 percent of U.S. per capita income is heavily influenced by the inclusion of China and India, which account for 40 percent of the world's population. But some other large countries—Bangladesh, Indonesia, Pakistan, the Philippines, and Thailand—are also in that category.

In some of the most populous countries, the distance behind the U.S. level of per capita output has been narrowing. The bottom chart shows the growth rate of per capita output between 1990 and 1996 in all countries with population exceeding 100 million. The growth rate for China is prominent, but the rate for India is also impressive. Judgments about the interpretation of Indonesia's rapid growth rate from 1990 to 1996 are complicated by that country's severe economic crisis in 1998. The drastic decline in Russian per capita income reflects the radical transformation of the economic and social system, with the future still in doubt.

HOW GDP PER CAPITA OF THE WORLD'S POPULATION COMPARES WITH U.S. GDP PER CAPITA, 1996

PERCENT OF WORLD POPULATION

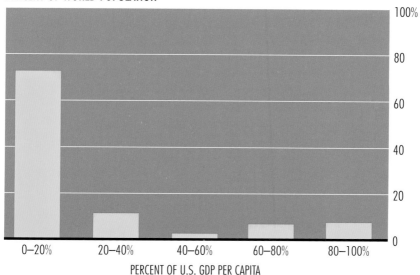

PERCENT OF U.S. GDP PER CAPITA

GROWTH OF GDP PER CAPITA, 1990–1996

ANNUAL RATE

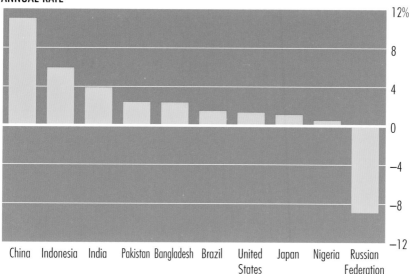

Since 1973, per capita output has grown less rapidly than earlier in our history.

The data for the earlier part of the period shown here are not sufficiently reliable to permit one to say with confidence that the growth rate of per capita GDP was lower from 1889 to 1929 than from 1929 to 1973. But growth after 1973 was probably lower than in the preceding years. Whether the growth from 1929 to 1973 or the slower growth after 1973 needs the explanation is hard to say.

The results for 1929–1948 are surprising, since that period includes the decade of the Great Depression, but the forced draft of the wartime economy evidently overcame the slow growth attributable to the depression. The period 1948–1973 also contained some exceptional features. There were still opportunities for investment and technological advance left over from the depression and the war; the educational attainment of the labor force advanced rapidly; and the American economy benefited from a significant opening to world trade.

The performance of the economy after 1973 was adversely affected by the connected factors of the inflation of that time, the recessions of 1974 and 1982, and the sharp increases in oil prices. At bottom, the slowdown in the growth of per capita output after 1973 was a reflection of the slowdown in the growth of productivity—of output per employed person—at the same time. The behavior of productivity is analyzed in part five of this volume.

GROWTH RATE OF U.S. REAL GDP PER CAPITA, 1889–1998

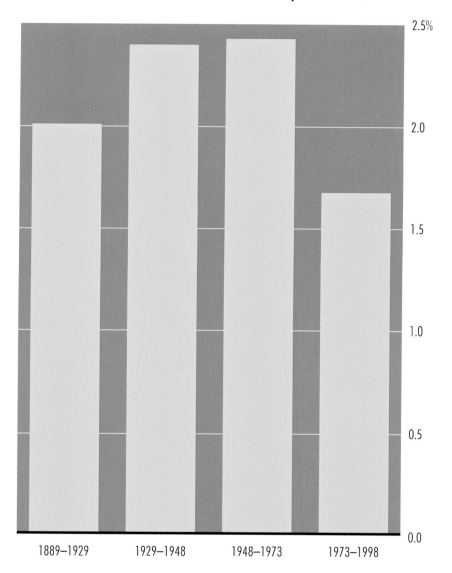

PART TWO

Uses of the National Output

Most of what we produce as a nation goes for personal consumption.

There are different ways of measuring what we produce as a nation. One measure —gross domestic product, or GDP— views total production, or output, as the sum of final demands: personal consumption, private investment, purchases by government at all levels (federal, state, and local), and purchases by foreigners (exports). The nation's total output can also be measured by adding up net output of every industry or by adding up all incomes earned in production. GDP as the sum of final demands is the best-known measure.

In 1998, 68 percent of total U.S. output measured in current dollars went to personal consumption expenditures. About 16 percent represented private domestic investment by business for machinery and equipment of all types; for the construction of factories, shopping centers, office buildings, and housing; and for additions to business inventories. Governments accounted for 18 percent of the output, while exports were 11 percent.

Those proportions add up to more than 100 percent of GDP. The excess is attributable to imports. In the typical statistical format for this country, imports are subtracted from exports to yield a category labeled *net exports*, but that is just one of several ways in which the figures might be presented. In 1998, with gross exports at 11 percent and gross imports at 13 percent, net exports were negative by slightly less than 2 percent. Showing exports and imports individually, as on the adjoining page, gives a clearer picture of the importance of all foreign trade to the U.S. economy.

SHARES OF GDP BY FINAL DEMAND CATEGORY, 1998

PERCENT OF TOTAL GDP IN CURRENT DOLLARS

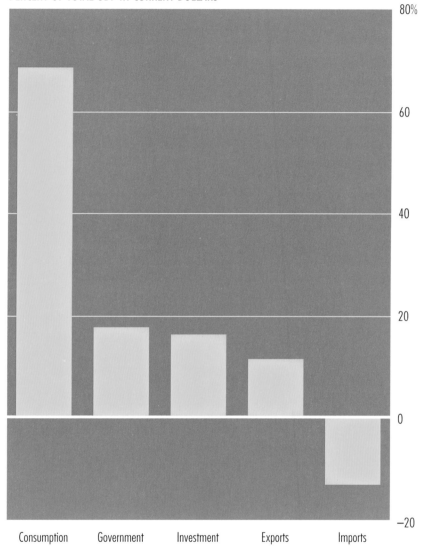

From 1950 to 1998, per capita real consumption expenditures increased at an average rate of 2 percent a year.

What is meant here by *personal consumption* is the expenditures of individuals and households—that is, excluding government and business—for their own use, except their purchases of houses. This concept differs substantially from other common-sense meanings of consumption.

On the one hand, it might be said that the entire output goes for personal consumption, either currently or in the future. Business investment and government investment in things such as roads are intended to increase future consumption. Government expenditures for national security are intended, among other objectives, to protect the present or future ability of the population to consume. Many other government expenditures provide services that are considered private consumption when paid for privately, such as medical care and education.

On the other hand, some expenditures included in consumption have characteristics of investment—education, for example, which increases the ability to earn income. Most consumer durables—automobiles, appliances, television, furniture—yield flows of services over long periods, measured in years. From an economic point of view, only the value of such flows in each year should be counted as personal consumption expenditures. In addition, some consumption expenditures could well be considered inputs in the production process—such as the food that supplies human energy, without which work could not be done.

Yet when all this has been said, the measured total of consumption expenditures is the best indication of the extent to which the output of the economy is currently contributing to the satisfaction of the wants of millions of individuals and households.

REAL CONSUMPTION EXPENDITURES PER CAPITA, 1950–1998

CHAINED 1992 DOLLARS

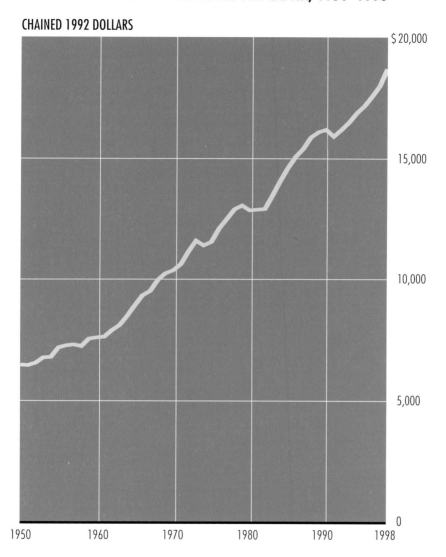

Since the 1950s, the personal consumption share of real GDP has risen, the private business investment share has been roughly stable, and the government share has declined.

The chart on the next page shows the changing percentage shares of real GDP since World War II. The data reflect the use of average prices in 1972, which is roughly midway between the earliest and most recent dates. These prices provide reasonable approximations of the changing distribution of real GDP and, for purposes of deflation, present a more balanced picture than would be provided by the use of prices in a more recent period. (See p. 280, the technical note.)

Many factors are responsible for the rising share of personal consumption of GDP. Consumption depends partly on personal after-tax income, which has increased relative to real GDP since the end of World War II—at least until recently. In turn, higher income reflects, among other things, a generally rising share of labor compensation in income and an increased importance of transfer payments. The rising stock market of the 1980s and 1990s has probably been an influence, although economists remain divided regarding the effect of the market on aggregate consumer spending.

Since World War II, private domestic investment in the United States has absorbed 13–20 percent of annual GDP—the lesser figure in recession years and the higher in booms. This short-run instability tends to even out over longer periods, as the chart demonstrates. Researchers who have analyzed data back to the nineteenth century have found comparative stability—aside from the business cycle—in the private saving share of GNP. The saving share of GNP is a reflection of the share of private investment in GNP, as we point out further on.

The government share has decreased. This refers to what is now called government consumption expenditures and government investment in the national income and product accounts, but not to the broader aggregate that embraces transfer payments. The share of federal defense purchases has been irregular but generally declining; the federal nondefense spending share has been fairly stable, while the state and local spending share has been rising.

The shares for exports and imports have changed the most over the postwar decades. One way of seeing the importance of foreign trade is by adding imports to exports instead of subtracting them. In the 1950s, the sum of exports and imports was about 8 percent, but from 1990 to 1998, it averaged 24 percent.

AVERAGE SHARES OF REAL GDP BY DECADE, 1950–1998

PERCENT, BASED ON CHAINED 1972 DOLLARS

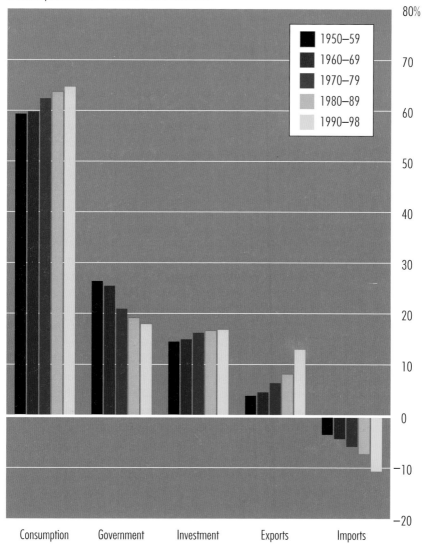

Since 1977, the share of food and beverages in personal consumption expenditures has declined, while the share of recreation has risen sharply.

The chart compares shares of expenditures for 1997 with those for 1977. The twelve categories embrace all personal consumption expenditures and reflect percentages based on chained 1987 dollars.

Over the twenty years, half the categories have increased in importance and half decreased. Only the food, beverage, and tobacco category has decreased substantially. The decline in the food and beverage share (including or excluding tobacco) illustrates one of the best-established laws in economics: as the income of families—or nations—increases, the proportion spent on food diminishes. The restaurant share of the grand total has also declined, but not as much as the share of food at home.

The increased proportion of spending for medical care reflects the sensitivity of medical spending to higher real incomes, the greater availability of new but costly medical procedures and drugs, and the increasing prevalence of medical insurance that weakens patients' incentives to economize on medical care. Because of difficulties with the price indexes, the increase in real medical care expenditures may well be understated (see page 242).

The share for recreation has almost doubled, excluding what is already classified as transportation, food, housing, and foreign travel. Although much of the rise reflects the huge growth of home computers, rising income and more leisure and retirement time have boosted other types of recreation expenditures. These are important factors in the large percentage increase in the share for foreign travel and in some of the rise in the share for clothing.

Long-term comparisons of this sort should be used with care, because they are subject to so many qualifications. Difficulties posed by the figures themselves are discussed on pages 252–63. Over and above this are problems associated with unmeasured benefits and costs. Although, for example, the importance of transportation expenditures has decreased slightly over the past twenty years, the statistics take no account of the benefits of the greater mobility or privacy that each individual has with an automobile at his disposal, or of the time saved traveling, or, for that matter, of the social costs of the pollution caused by widespread automobile use.

DISTRIBUTION OF CONSUMPTION EXPENDITURES, 1977 AND 1997

PERCENT OF TOTAL CONSUMPTION IN CHAINED 1987 DOLLARS

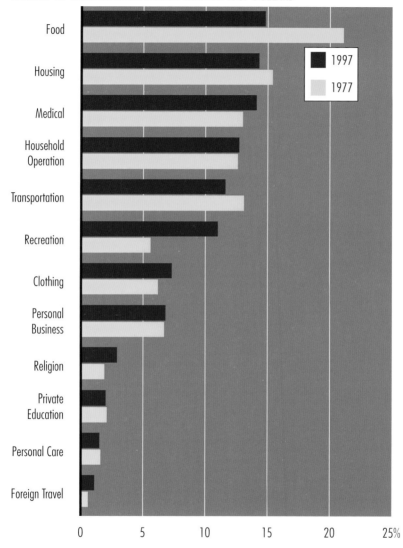

PART THREE

Who Produces the National Output?

Since the early 1950s, the business sector has increased in importance, while the government sector has declined.

Consumers buy most of what the nation produces, but who produces the product? To answer this question, the Commerce Department distinguishes three sectors of the domestic economy: business, government, and private households and institutions. The sectors are unequal in size, as the pie chart shows. Most output in the United States is produced in the business sector, which by these definitions accounted for 85 percent of the total in 1998. The business total is somewhat exaggerated because of the peculiarities of classification in the national income and product accounts. The shelter and amenities of living provided by housing are classified as services. The services of owner-occupied homes, which accounted for 6 percent of GDP, are included as part of the business product.

Under this classification, government is measured by the pay of government civilian employees and members of the armed forces plus the consumption of government-owned capital. The latter is an annual allowance for the wear and tear on our highways, public buildings, and government-owned equipment of all types. The computers, missiles, buildings, and desks bought by governments are produced in the business sector.

Shares based on constant 1972 dollars appear in the bottom chart. Owner-occupied housing has been removed from business and is displayed separately.

 Despite the increased role of government in the economy in the second half of the twentieth century, the business share has risen, while the government share has declined. The rise in the business share would be somewhat greater if not for the decline in the importance of farms.

Households now produce one-tenth of 1 percent of total output. The output of households measures work done by cooks, servants, gardeners, nursemaids, and the like. Some work previously done by household workers is now done by business, but some has never been part of measured U.S. GDP insofar as it is work done mainly by housewives, increasingly with household appliances. (This issue is discussed further on pages 258 and 260.)

Nonprofit organizations, which include private colleges and universities and not-for-profit hospitals, accounted for 4.5 percent of GDP in 1998. Since the early postwar years, the growth of their output, as well as their prices, has been considerably above average.

SHARES OF GDP BY PRODUCING SECTOR, 1998

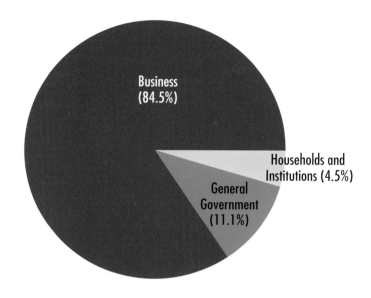

Business
(84.5%)

Households and
Institutions (4.5%)

General
Government
(11.1%)

SHARES OF REAL GDP BY PRODUCING SECTOR, 1948–1997

PERCENT OF TOTAL (IN CHAINED 1972 DOLLARS)

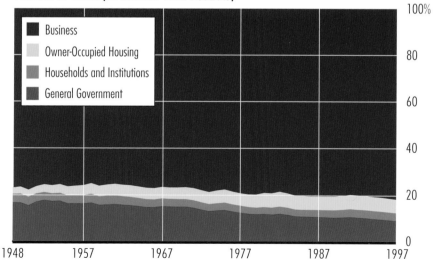

■ Business
□ Owner-Occupied Housing
■ Households and Institutions
■ General Government

The share of domestic production accounted for by service industries has risen faster than average at least since 1977.

It is often said that America has become a service economy. That statement can be looked at from two different points of view: in terms of final demands for services and in terms of industries supplying services.

In 1998, 54.5 percent of current-dollar GDP reflected final demands for services as distinct from goods and construction. This was much more than the service proportion of 32 percent in 1948. Over this half-century, the increased proportion based on current dollars reflects a much greater than average rise in service prices and a slightly greater than average rise in physical volume. Increases in real spending on services occurred in the consumer sector, in exports (net of imports), and in state and local government employment, partly offset, especially in recent decades, by declines in national defense employment. The top chart shows postwar shares of real GDP based on 1972 prices. Measuring the split between the change in physical volume and the change in prices is complicated by difficulties in measuring many service prices.

The statement can also be looked at in relation to the industries that provide services for the economy. The consumer who buys a refrigerator, a final demand, has acquired some output of many "service" industries—transportation, retailing, wholesaling, real estate, and finance—as well as of those industries ordinarily referred to as service industries, such as advertising and accounting. In these terms, the number of broad industry divisions that supply goods—as distinct from services—is small: agriculture, forestry, and fisheries; mining; construction; and manufacturing. On this basis, all other industry divisions are classified as services.

Data for each industry's contribution to the nation's production are available on a consistent basis since 1977. In real terms (1987 dollars),

- The share of the nation's domestic private production accounted for by service-producing industries rose from about 65 percent in 1977 to 70.5 percent in 1997 (see bottom chart). Since government is 100 percent services under this definition, including government would raise the current service share but dampen its increase.
- The manufacturing share of private GDP fell during the 1980s and early 1990s but has recovered. Its share of real private GDP in 1997 was as high as it was in 1977.
- Mining and construction grew less than average, and agriculture more than average, since 1977.

SHARES OF REAL TOTAL OUTPUT BY TYPE OF PRODUCT, 1948–1998

BASED ON CHAINED 1972 DOLLARS

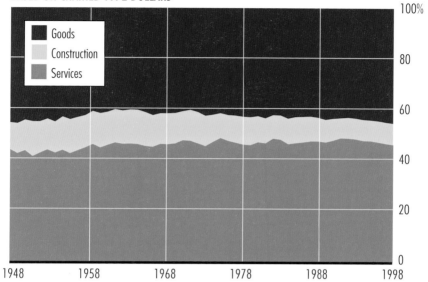

Legend:
- Goods
- Construction
- Services

y-axis: 100%, 80, 60, 40, 20, 0

x-axis: 1948, 1958, 1968, 1978, 1988, 1998

SHARES OF REAL TOTAL OUTPUT BY PRODUCING INDUSTRIES, 1977–1997

BASED ON CHAINED 1987 DOLLARS

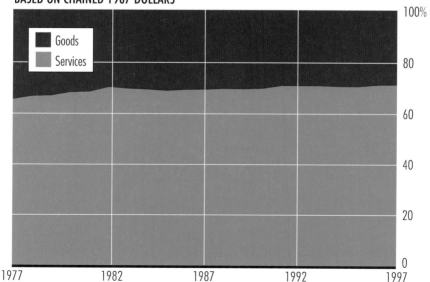

Legend:
- Goods
- Services

y-axis: 100%, 80, 60, 40, 20, 0

x-axis: 1977, 1982, 1987, 1992, 1997

Although pay in the service industries is below average, this category embraces many industries with above-average pay.

There is a common perception that the exceptionally rapid growth of employment in service industries means only one thing, namely, exceptionally rapid growth in low-paid industries. Service industries are a diverse group that includes legal and financial services, health services, transportation, and public utilities. The average wage of workers in all service industries in 1997 was about 94 percent of the average in all private industries (top chart). Over the past decade, this ratio has changed little.

About 43 percent of all service workers in 1997 were employed in industries whose average wage exceeded the national average, the highest being security and commodity brokers at $136,324. Services, in contrast with goods-producing industries, embrace more industries in which pay is below the U.S. average for all employees. Of thirty-three service industries listed by the Commerce Department, thirteen paid below the average for all private industries in 1997. These thirteen accounted for 57 percent of private service employment and 41 percent of total private employment. An important part of the below-average group is retail trade, with pay at only 58 percent of the average.

ANNUAL COMPENSATION IN SERVICE INDUSTRIES AND ALL PRIVATE INDUSTRIES, 1997

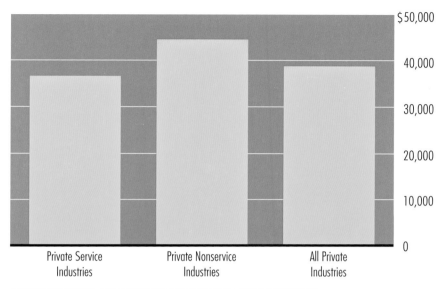

Private Service Industries	Private Nonservice Industries	All Private Industries

DISTRIBUTION OF SERVICE INDUSTRY EMPLOYMENT, BY COMPENSATION LEVEL, 1997

PERCENT OF SERVICE INDUSTRY EMPLOYMENT

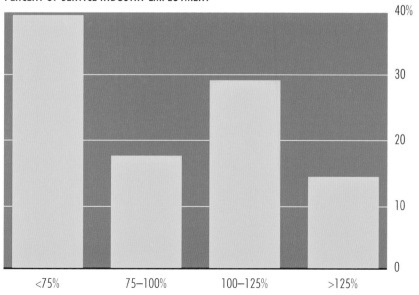

Compensation as a percentage of all private industry average.

Except during the depression years, the farm share of total output has declined in the twentieth century.

Over the past century, farm production has increased, but production in industry and in other parts of the economy has grown much faster. From 1929 to 1998, GDP increased at an annual rate of 3.3 percent, while the corresponding figure for farm output has been 2.0 percent. Today, farm business accounts for about 1 percent of our GDP, whereas one hundred years ago the proportion (measured in 1929 prices) was about 23 percent. America was predominantly a farm economy in its early years; industrialization made its most rapid gains after the middle of the nineteenth century.

The growth in agricultural production was accompanied by dramatic decreases in the labor resources employed, as the farm population was attracted by better-paying jobs in industry. Farm output kept rising, because farmers employed more equipment, while greater use of fertilizer, better seed and pesticides, and improved farming methods—the products of research—raised productivity.

The farm experience observable in this country can be seen elsewhere in the industrialized world—except that, in the last quarter of the twentieth century, the relative importance of farming has declined more sharply in other industrialized countries than in the United States. Today, agriculture contributes little to GDP in the leading industrialized nations. The shift from farming to more productive activities explains a sizable fraction of total productivity gains. The United States realized these benefits earlier than other countries, but farming is now such a limited activity in the industrialized world that the further gains from moving resources from farms into industry are slight.

FARM PRODUCTION AND TOTAL GDP, 1933–1998

INDEXES: 1992=100

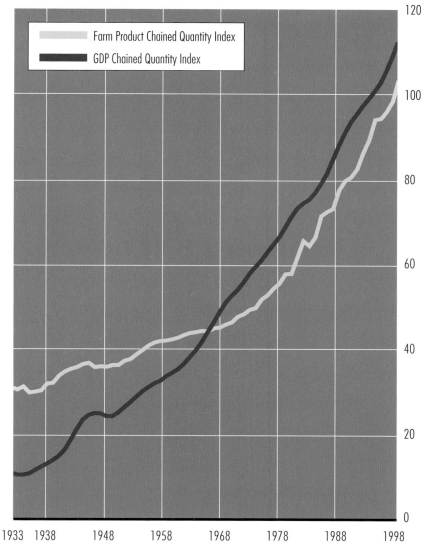

Note: Data plotted are five-year moving averages centered on the last year. First plotting point is 1933.

PART FOUR

Distribution of the National Income

Gross product is only one way of measuring what we produce as a nation. Net product and national income are valid alternatives.

Most people are familiar with the gross measures of production, such as GNP and now GDP, but many economists think that the net measures are superior. In this context, the difference between gross and net is depreciation—capital used up in current production—and destruction of capital, by things such as earthquakes and floods. One may ask why the value of current production should include the value of capital used up in that production if GDP is a value-added concept. There is a practical answer. Net product would be the most prominent measure of total production except that, in the absence of the necessary data years ago, the Commerce Department took a long time to develop an appropriate set of depreciation figures. During that development period, the gross measures became well established.

Another, and equally valid, way of measuring the net value of output arrives at a total by adding up all the costs of production. That sum is the national income. The relevant costs are the earnings of the factors of production. The sum of these earnings—wages, salaries, fringe benefits, rents, and interest, as well as profits and losses—in principle yields the same total value measured in terms of final products, that is, by personal consumption, private investment, government consumption and investment, and exports, with certain qualifications. The value of products purchased in final markets includes depreciation as well as excise and sales taxes, whereas the income shares do not. Income includes the value of government subsidies, however, which is not part of the value of products. The chart shows in condensed form the relationship between the gross national product and national income. For simplicity, the small adjustments that would show only gross domestic product and gross domestic income are not illustrated.

Long-term growth rates are almost identical, whether output is measured from the product side or from the income side. Differences show up over short periods, partly because of differing data sources.

GROSS NATIONAL PRODUCT, NET NATIONAL PRODUCT, AND NATIONAL INCOME, 1998

TRILLIONS OF DOLLARS

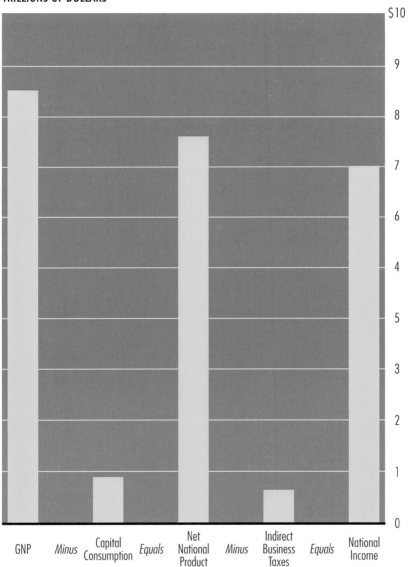

| GNP | Minus | Capital Consumption | Equals | Net National Product | Minus | Indirect Business Taxes | Equals | National Income |

About 70 percent of the national income is compensation of employees. The share has risen over the long run but has drifted down since the 1970s.

The divisions of income observable in the national income statistics are determined by the availability of the data. The pie chart shows the distribution in 1998 according to the official national income accounts. The labor share (employee compensation) in that year was 71.2 percent of the national income, while corporate profits before taxes were 11.8 percent. The remainder went to proprietors' income, net interest, and rental income of persons.

From an economic point of view, the classifications are not clean. The labor share, for example, includes what many economists consider a return on investment, that is, the investment made in the worker's education. The payrolls of some companies include employees with unique technical and managerial skills who make important contributions to company profits. Proprietors' income, which was 8.3 percent of the national income in 1998, in principle reflects what unincorporated businessmen earned as labor (wages and salaries) and what—if anything—may have been left over in the form of profits.

Other shares of the national income have their own peculiar problems. Corporate profits reflect the definitions of the Bureau of Economic Analysis; these involve several inflation adjustments to the so-called book profits that corporations report to their stockholders in financial reports. The adjusted figures are superior to the book figures for most purposes, but the adjustments are arbitrary to some extent. Net interest, unlike profits, contains no inflation adjustment, although many analysts think that it should, because the comparatively high interest rates of the 1980s, for example, contain an *inflation premium*. Most of what is really rent appears as corporate profits, because the owners of land are mainly corporations.

Whether compared with 1929 or the early post–World War II period, the employee compensation share of national income has risen dramatically. It has declined slightly since the 1980s.

PERCENTAGE DISTRIBUTION OF NATIONAL INCOME, 1998

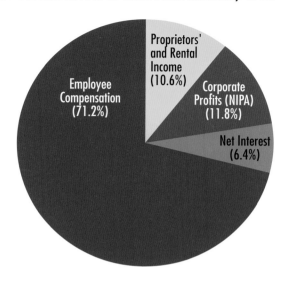

EMPLOYEE COMPENSATION AS PERCENTAGE
OF NATIONAL INCOME, 1929–1998

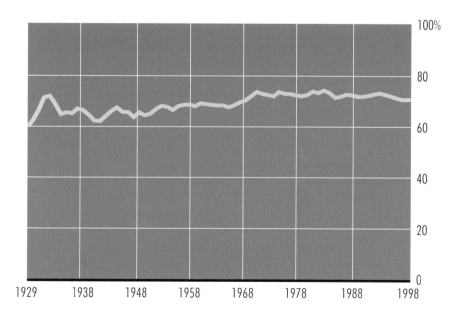

The proportion of the national income for fringe benefits has risen, while the wage and salary share is about the same as in 1929.

As a share of employee compensation, fringe benefits grew especially rapidly in the 1950s, 1960s, and 1970s and at a slower rate since then. In 1998, seventeen cents of every dollar of employee compensation represented fringes.

When compared with national income, as distinct from employee compensation, fringe benefits have risen from less than 1 percent in 1929 to almost 12 percent in 1998 (top chart). They were close to 14 percent in 1993. In contrast, the wage and salary portion of national income has not changed much since 1929. It was 58.4 percent in that year and 59.4 percent in 1998, although from the 1950s through the 1970s, the wage and salary share was about 63 percent.

Fringe benefits, or contributions by employers, are of two types: those required by law—such as Social Security and unemployment compensation—and those made by employers for private pension, health benefits, and similar plans (middle chart). Benefits required by law—"employer contributions for social insurance"—rose faster than national income after World War II as a result of higher tax rates and increases in wages covered under Social Security; new programs such as Medicare in the mid-1960s; and expanded benefits to public employees, especially state and local. Growth of this share of the national income leveled off in the mid-1980s at about 6 percent and has declined a little since.

The other part of fringe benefits—private pension and benefit plans—grew even faster than mandated programs. In 1959, public and private programs were about the same size, each around 2.6 percent of national income. By 1993, the private component was more than 7 percent, but it has fallen by more than a full percentage point since then.

Earlier, pensions were the commonest type of private programs, but they were soon surpassed by contributions for health (bottom chart). From 1969 to 1993, employer contributions for health accounted for almost all the rise in private plans. In 1993, private contributions by employers for health were 4.7 percent of the national income. All major types of contributions have fallen since 1993, but the health share has fallen the most.

Recent research has shown that as income taxes rise, employees prefer to obtain tax-free benefits from their employers, rather than taxable wages and salaries, and to shift toward noncontributory plans and away from benefit plans in which the worker contributes (see part fourteen).

TOTAL EMPLOYEE COMPENSATION—WAGES, SALARIES, AND FRINGES— AS PERCENTAGE OF NATIONAL INCOME, 1929–1998

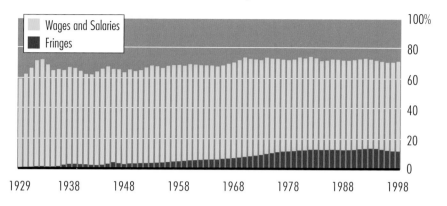

FRINGE BENEFITS AS PERCENTAGE OF NATIONAL INCOME BY TYPE, 1959–1998

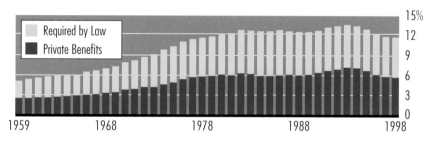

EMPLOYER CONTRIBUTIONS TO PRIVATE PENSIONS AND OTHER BENEFITS AS PERCENTAGE OF NATIONAL INCOME, 1959–1997

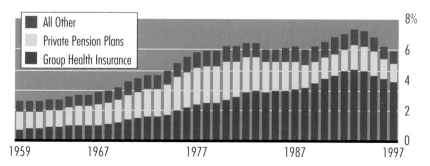

Note: "All other" includes supplementary unemployment compensation, workers' compensation, and group life insurance.

The share of the national income for interest has fallen from its peaks in the 1980s.

In the national accounts, measurement of interest poses many difficulties that can only be touched on here. Net interest in the national income refers solely to the interest paid by business. As such, it includes interest paid by individuals on their home mortgages and home improvements, because homeowners in the national accounts are treated as businesses. Government interest is excluded on the theory that it does not arise from current production; it is viewed as a transfer payment.

The significance of "net" in net interest is that interest received by business is subtracted from interest paid by business. Net interest in 1998 was $449 billion, or 6.4 percent of the national income, but this was the difference between roughly $2.1 trillion in interest paid and $1.7 trillion in interest received. Inflation affects both sides, but not necessarily to the same extent. Interest rates peaked in the first half of the 1980s. The peak share of national income came later—1989—partly because it took some time before homeowners refinanced their mortgages and businessmen their outstanding debt.

Economists often view the nominal or observed interest rate as consisting of two main parts: an underlying "real" rate, which would prevail in a noninflationary economy, and an inflation premium that fluctuates with the expected rate of inflation. If tomorrow's inflation rate is expected to be the same as today's, then today's real rate of interest is today's nominal rate of interest minus today's rate of inflation. Some economists maintain that the interest share of the national income would not have risen so much in the 1970s and 1980s if the inflation premium implicit in a nominal interest rate were removed from the calculation of net interest. This operation would be analogous to the inflation adjustment made for profits (see page 48). Calculating that inflation adjustment poses difficulties, however, mainly because the expected rate of inflation cannot be observed and need not be the same as today's actual rate—or some average of the recent past. Even so, there can be little doubt that the high rates of interest from about 1976 to 1984 reflected high expected rates of inflation.

NET INTEREST AS PERCENTAGE OF NATIONAL INCOME, 1929–1998

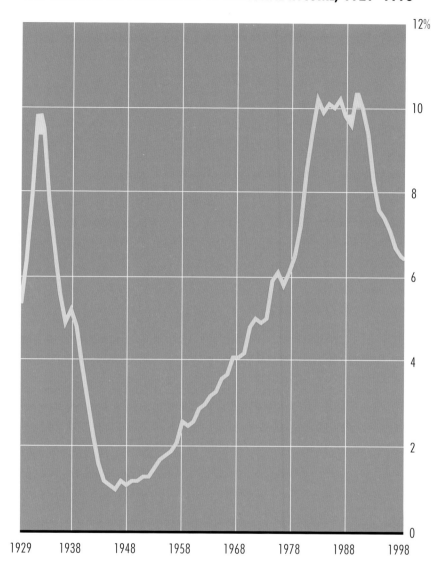

Despite the decline in the 1990s, the share for interest is higher than it was from the early 1950s to the late 1970s.

One reason for the increase in the interest share is that, in relative terms, business is using much more debt than it did, as shown on the facing page. The top chart shows how the ratio of credit market debt to national income has risen since the end of World War II. The ratio has increased rapidly since 1993. Credit market debt, on which interest is normally paid, excludes liabilities such as income tax payables and trade payables.

Economists do not fully understand why the share remained high long after interest rates plummeted in the 1980s. Part of the answer is found in innovations in the financial field such as various kinds of "hedging devices"—options, futures, and the like—which provide protection against interest rate changes and have encouraged greater use of debt. Leveraged buyouts, so prominent in the 1980s, increased the volume of debt in relation to income.

The bottom chart, showing the yield on a U.S. Treasury note with a constant ten-year maturity, illustrates the rise and decline in interest rates. (The pattern is quite similar to the pattern of a high-grade corporate bond on an annual basis.) This particular series peaked in 1981 and declined irregularly through 1998.

The other line in the bottom chart illustrates the ratio of gross interest paid by nonfinancial corporations to the credit market debt of those corporations. This ratio is an average interest rate that reflects not only the rates at which business borrowed but also the changing mixture of debt maturities. The interesting point about this second line is how its broad contours resemble the constant-maturity interest rate illustrated by the Treasury note. One possible explanation for the similarity is that the mixture of corporate debt and the relative spreads among different maturities of debt have not changed radically. Some change, however, has occurred. Since the mid-1980s, the increased relative importance of long-term debt would explain some widening evident in the second chart. Also, the overhang of existing debt that is not refinanced tends to dampen the fall in the ratio of interest to outstanding debt.

RATIO OF CREDIT MARKET DEBT TO NATIONAL INCOME, 1945–1998

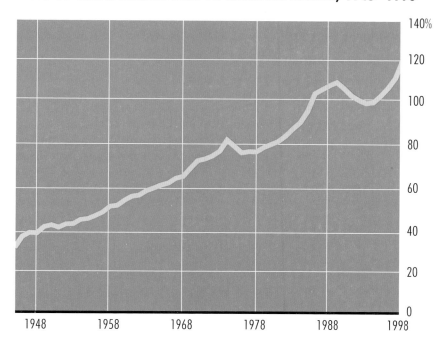

RATIO OF INTEREST PAID TO DEBT, NONFINANCIAL CORPORATIONS, 1953–1997

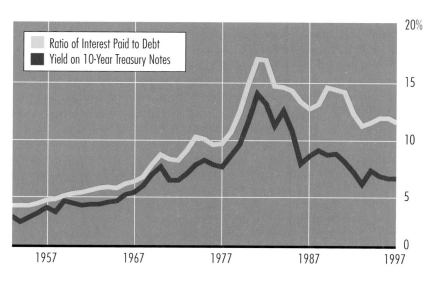

Ratio of Interest Paid to Debt
Yield on 10-Year Treasury Notes

In 1996–1998, corporate profits after taxes as a share of the national income approached the high points in the post–World War II period.

Because corporate profits are highly sensitive to changing business conditions, the share of profits in national income undergoes pronounced changes over the business cycle. Although employment drops when sales and orders fall, wage rates are rarely cut. Overhead, much of which is payroll, changes slowly. Businesses find profit margins squeezed. In contrast, in the early stages of a recovery, profits tend to rise rapidly, because costs change little while sales are increasing.

The cyclical variability of profits is a well-known phenomenon, but less well known—or understood—is the changing share of profits over the postwar years. In the 1950s and 1960s, corporate profits before taxes as a share of national income averaged 13 percent; over the next two decades, they averaged 8–10 percent. The 1990s, especially the years 1995–1998, have witnessed some recovery in the profits share.

One explanation of the relatively poor performance of profits in the 1970s and 1980s concerns the unusual character of the early postwar years following the depressed 1930s and war-affected 1940s. In this view, demand was unusually strong after the war, and it was inevitable that profit shares would shrink once the abnormal components of demand disappeared. In addition, in the early years, there was relatively little competition from Western Europe and Japan, which were recovering from the war. Once industrialized foreign economies recovered, competition intensified, and domestic producers found it necessary to cut both margins and costs to maintain market shares.

The recovery in the profit share evident in the mid-1990s may well reflect the effects of the severe cost-cutting and downsizing by large American firms in the 1980s and early 1990s. From 1996 to 1998, profits before taxes as a share of national income were still clearly lower than in the 1950s and 1960s, but because taxes on corporate profits had been cut relative to income, the after-tax shares were only slightly below the highs of the mid-1960s.

CORPORATE PROFITS BEFORE AND AFTER TAXES AS PERCENTAGES OF NATIONAL INCOME, 1929–1998

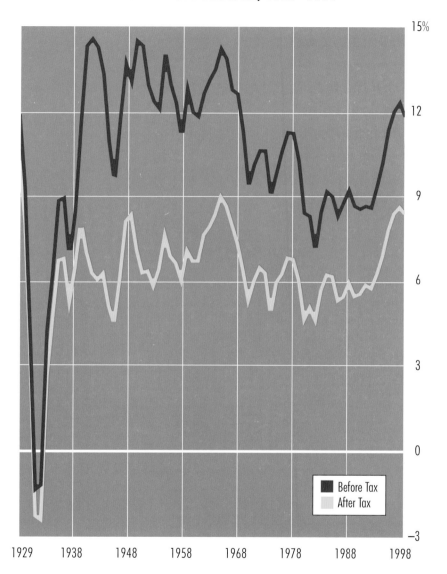

Note: NIPA definition of profits.

Stockholder reports of profits can be misleading. During inflationary periods, they may understate the cost of goods sold and depreciation. The national income version of profits adjusts for these and other distortions.

When prices are rising, the profits that appear in reports to stockholders ("book profits") will be overstated if companies use conventional accounting methods. Under these methods, the costs of goods sold that appear on the books do not fully reflect the costs at which the goods were acquired; as a consequence, reported profits are too high. Companies pay taxes on these overstated profits. As the rate of inflation rose in the 1970s, companies turned increasingly to accounting methods that gave a truer picture of their profits. In measuring profits for national income purposes, however, the Commerce Department has always made an *inventory valuation adjustment* to remove this inflationary distortion.

A problem caused by inflation also arises in the calculation of depreciation. Companies typically carry on their books assets such as plants and equipment at historical cost; they figure depreciation on the basis of these costs. But when prices rise, the depreciation calculated at the lower price will fall short of the amount needed to replace, say, an old machine with a new one. As an element of cost, depreciation so measured is too low; as a result, reported profits are too high. The Commerce Department makes an adjustment for this distortion also, the so-called *capital consumption adjustment.* Finally, changing IRS regulations regarding how depreciation is determined have introduced further distortions. The Commerce Department calculates depreciation on a standard basis so that distortion will not affect profits for national income purposes.

The chart shows the two versions of profits. In the period of high inflation—from the early 1970s to the early 1980s—book profits were consistently overstated relative to national income and product accounts (NIPA) profits, because book profits included inventory profits and reflected abnormally low depreciation charges. Since 1983, book profits have been understated relative to national income profits, partly because inventory profits declined but mainly because depreciation allowances were liberalized under the tax laws.

NIPA AND STOCKHOLDER VERSIONS OF PROFITS AS PERCENTAGES OF NATIONAL INCOME, 1970–1998

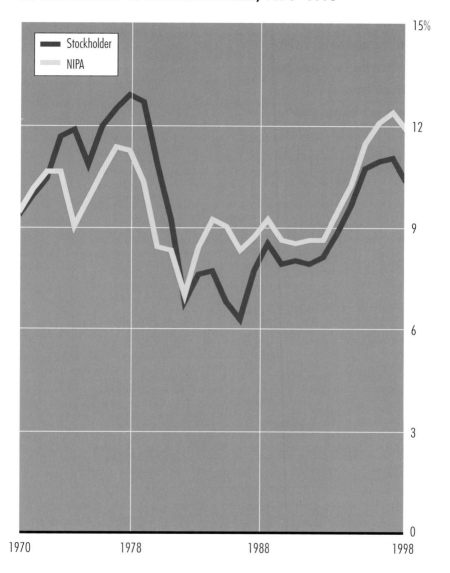

For nonfinancial corporations, the after-tax return— profits and interest— on tangible capital has averaged 5.8 percent since 1959.

Since profits and interest are returns to capital, it is instructive to view their combined total in relation to capital. The charts on the opposite page show the experience of nonfinancial corporations since 1959. Nonfinancial corporations provide a superior basis for determining the return on capital, because the distinction between labor income and capital income is better defined in a corporation. In a sole proprietorship or partnership, profit includes some income attributable to the owner's labor, but just how much can only be estimated.

The numerator consists of profits—as defined in the national income and product accounts—plus net interest, minus corporate profits taxes. Profits could also be measured as they are in reports to stockholders, as was illustrated on pages 49, and before taxes as well. The denominator refers to net reproducible tangible assets of these same corporations. In this context, *reproducible tangible assets* refer to buildings, equipment, and inventories. Land and minerals in the ground are excluded. The term *net* means that assets are valued after depreciation has been deducted. The assets are valued at replacement cost, and not at historical or book cost (the cost at which the assets were acquired). Numerator and denominator thus reflect the same price level, although what is really needed for assets is current value, the price at which these assets—most of which are not new—would sell on the market. Current cost is only an approximation of current value. Further on, we discuss other difficulties in measuring capital.

Since 1959, the after-tax return on tangible capital (excluding land) has averaged about 5.75 percent. Returns were highest in the 1960s, fell sharply in the 1970s, and have risen since then. From 1995 to 1998, returns were close to the highest years of the 1960s (top chart).

The return on capital can be factored into two parts: (1) the share of profits and net interest in total domestic income of these corporations and (2) the income produced per dollar of net capital stock. The share of profits and interest before taxes in corporate income—the property share—has fluctuated around a flat trend since the early 1970s. After taxes, however, the trend is upward (middle chart). This trend has been reinforced by the movement of income produced per dollar of net capital. The income-to-capital ratio fell from the 1960s to the recession in the early 1980s, but since then has risen (bottom chart).

RATE OF RETURN ON TANGIBLE CAPITAL, NONFINANCIAL CORPORATIONS, 1959–1998

PERCENT OF TANGIBLE CAPITAL

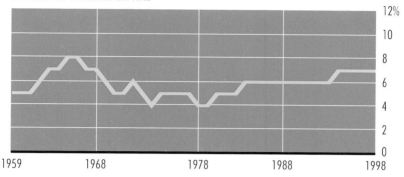

Note: NIPA definition of profits after taxes.

PROPERTY INCOME'S SHARE OF DOMESTIC INCOME, 1959–1998

PERCENT OF DOMESTIC INCOME

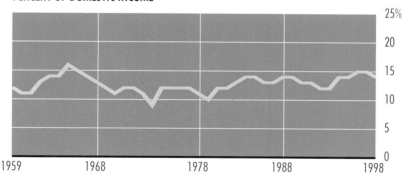

Note: NIPA definition of profits after taxes.

RATIO OF DOMESTIC INCOME TO CAPITAL, 1959–1998

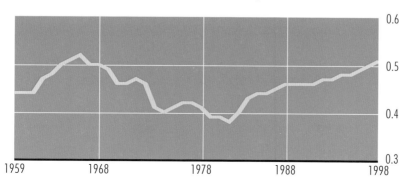

PART FIVE

Productivity

Over the long run, the increase in real output has exceeded the increase in the input of labor or the combined increase in the inputs of labor and capital. Output per unit of input is called *productivity*.

In 1997, America's real gross domestic business product was more than five times its level fifty years earlier. What was behind the production increase? To what extent did it reflect the use of more factors of production or inputs—the number of persons employed and the amount of capital that they had to work with—and to what extent did it reflect greater efficiency in the use of inputs, that is, increased productivity? We are interested in measuring productivity growth because rising productivity is what underlies rising living standards and most of what we think of as economic progress. If the rise in productivity slows down, so will the rise in living standards.

The top chart shows the basic facts about the growth of output and inputs in the private business sector from 1948 to 1997, as compiled by the Bureau of Labor Statistics. Typically, the growth of output is compared with the growth of labor input, which is measured in simplest terms by changes in employment and in hours worked per year. From 1948 to 1997, business output grew at an annual rate of 3.4 percent. Despite some decline in average hours, strong increases in employment (including the self-employed) brought about an average annual rise in labor input of 1.1 percent. Those changes suggest a labor productivity rise of 2.3 percent per year (3.4 − 1.1).

This particular measure, while useful, fails to note the presence of other factors that contribute to production—specifically, plants, equipment, inventories, and land. A more comprehensive measure of input prepared by the BLS takes account of these capital inputs as well. Labor and capital are combined with weights that reflect the shares of income produced. Since labor gets most of the national income, its weight is much larger than the weight of capital.

Over the postwar years, combined capital and labor inputs grew more than labor inputs alone; that is, labor had increasing amounts of capital to work with. But the combined inputs also grew less rapidly than output: 2.1 percent per year compared with 3.4 percent for output. With inputs measured on a more comprehensive basis, total factor, or multifactor, productivity grew at an annual rate of 1.3 percent (3.4 − 2.1). Over this half-century, multifactor productivity growth has been an important part of the growth of output.

The bottom chart makes explicit the productivity advances suggested by the information in the top chart.

TOTAL OUTPUT, LABOR HOURS, AND COMBINED INPUTS FOR PRIVATE BUSINESS, 1948–1997

INDEXES: 1948=100

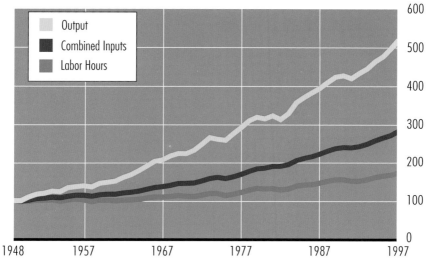

TWO MEASURES OF PRODUCTIVITY FOR PRIVATE BUSINESS, 1948–1997

INDEXES: 1948=100

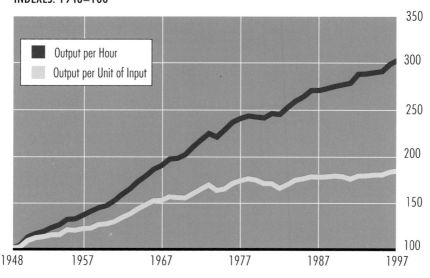

The rise in the educational levels of workers has contributed to the growth in output.

The increased education of the work force has been an important source of growth since at least the early twentieth century. As recently as 1969, 38 percent of the civilian labor force between ages twenty-five and sixty-four did not have a high school diploma; by 1998, that proportion had fallen to 11 percent. In 1969, 14 percent of the same labor force had a college degree or some graduate education; by 1998, that proportion had risen to 30 percent (top chart).

Educational attainment and earnings go together. In 1997, a male full-time year-round worker (eighteen years or older) whose education had ended with high school graduation earned 41 percent more than a man who had attended high school but had no diploma. In 1997, a man with a bachelor's degree earned 77 percent more than a man with a high school diploma (middle chart). The picture for women is roughly the same.

Most economists in this field believe that individuals with higher education levels earn more because they produce more. Education brings more skill and knowledge to the individual. The more educated a person, the greater variety of tasks he can perform and the greater the awareness of other job opportunities. A contrary view maintains that high school diplomas and college degrees are credentials, useful for hiring but not necessarily measures of what people actually produce on the job once hired. The employer who sees a young person with a degree is likely to view the individual as well motivated and reliable, that is, likelier to have characteristics considered desirable in an employee than an individual without a degree. The researcher trying to isolate a pure "education effect" on output is hampered by the difficulty of measuring personal characteristics and by the fact that other attributes, such as experience, are closely related to education.

Earnings differences by educational attainment have widened since the 1980s; that is an important development in recent history. Among men aged eighteen years or more with year-round full-time jobs, average incomes of those with an advanced degree rose more than the incomes of those with only a bachelor's degree, which rose more than the incomes of those with only a high school diploma. The bottom chart compares growth rates in incomes by education from 1979 to 1990 with those from 1991 to 1997. For men with an advanced degree, the rate of increase did not change, but for the other two groups, the rise decelerated.

PERCENTAGE OF CIVILIAN LABOR FORCE AGED TWENTY-FIVE TO SIXTY-FOUR, BY EDUCATIONAL ATTAINMENT, 1970–1998

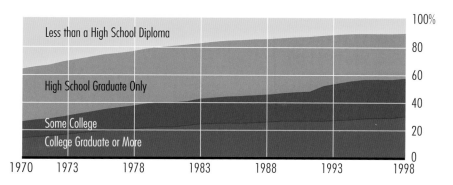

MEAN INCOMES OF MEN EIGHTEEN AND OLDER WHO WORK FULL-TIME YEAR-ROUND, BY EDUCATIONAL ATTAINMENT, 1997

INDEX: HIGH SCHOOL DIPLOMA=100

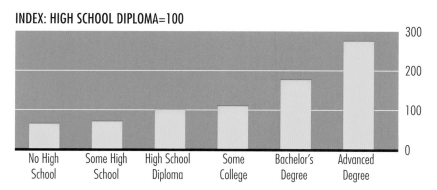

ANNUAL GROWTH IN THE MEAN INCOME OF MEN EIGHTEEN AND OLDER WHO WORK FULL-TIME YEAR-ROUND, BY EDUCATIONAL ATTAINMENT, 1979–1997

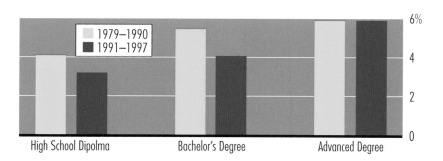

Increased tangible capital per labor hour has been an important source of rising labor productivity. All types of tangible capital have increased.

Capital can be viewed in many different ways. In the past half-century, most economists who have analyzed sources of growth have taken a conventional view of capital inputs as consisting of the services of structures, equipment, inventories, and land owned by private business. Government capital has usually been excluded. Most investigators have also excluded intangible capital such as human capital. Education and experience are forms of human capital. However, in studies accounting for growth, their influence has usually been treated as an enhancement of labor input. The top chart, incorporating data from the Bureau of Labor Statistics, shows how real tangible private capital and its components have increased since 1948.

The various types of tangible capital shown at the top are combined by the BLS into a single figure for all tangible capital services. The bottom chart shows this total for capital services per hour of labor worked (including hours of proprietors) in index form.

From 1948 to 1997, capital services per hour of labor rose at an annual rate of 2.5 percent. How much did this increase affect the rise in output per hour? The contribution that an input makes to the growth of output depends on two things: how much the input has grown and the importance, or weight, of the input. Input weights are commonly based on the shares in the national income produced by private business. Capital has a weight of about 31 percent, while labor receives about 69 percent of the income produced in the private business sector. The capital weight (0.31) times the annual rate of increase in capital services per labor hour (2.5) gives a contribution of 0.8 percent per year for tangible capital. Output per hour of labor rose at an annual rate of 2.3 percent. Thus, the increased capital per labor hour or the increased capital intensity of production accounted for 35 percent of the rise in output per hour (0.8/2.3).

Some economists question the appropriateness of using shares of the national income to weight the factor inputs. The market has many imperfections, so that labor receives income that might otherwise go to capital; as pointed out on page 38, the income classifications are not clean. Small changes in weights would not alter these results very much. Tangible capital makes an important contribution to the rise in output, but it is not the whole explanation of its growth.

PRODUCTIVE CAPITAL STOCK, PRIVATE BUSINESS, 1948–1997

TRILLIONS OF 1992 DOLLARS

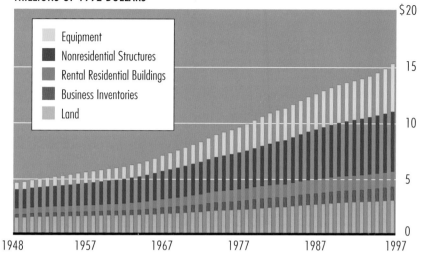

Legend:
- Equipment
- Nonresidential Structures
- Rental Residential Buildings
- Business Inventories
- Land

PRIVATE BUSINESS CAPITAL PER LABOR HOUR, 1948–1997

INDEX: 1948=100

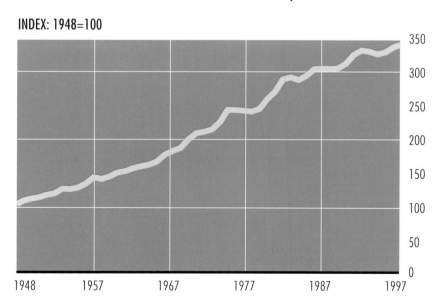

Private capital owned by business is only part of the nation's capital stock.

Government at all levels holds substantial stocks of capital in the form of school buildings, dams, and superhighways, as well as trucks, computers, and filing cabinets. Consumers also hold large stocks of durable assets such as automobiles, household appliances, furniture, boats, and consumer electronics. This so-called reproducible capital excludes land and mineral rights.

The chart plots for the years 1959–1997 the distribution of net stocks of fixed reproducible capital held by private business, government, and consumers, measured in chained 1992 dollars. End-of-1997 inventories held by business ($1.3 trillion in 1992 prices) and by government should be included, but are excluded here. The grand total of fixed capital at the end of 1997 was about $22 trillion in 1992 prices. Since 1959, the real stock has grown about as fast as net domestic product. The private residential and nonresidential shares of the stock have been fairly stable and doubtless reflect the long-term stability of private investment and its composition relative to GDP. The state and local share rose until the early 1970s, but has since fallen; the declining share reflects the slow growth in the public infrastructure. The federal government share is lower as a result of changes in military spending, while the consumer share has risen substantially, as consumers have bought more and more automobiles and other durables. At the end of 1997, government and consumer stocks were 31 percent of this aggregate. Private housing was an additional one-third of the total.

The services yielded by private business capital are part of GDP and are measured by the income earned in the form of profits, interest, and rents and depreciation. But this is not true of the services of durable goods held by consumers as the U.S. national income and product accounts are now defined. Consumer stocks provide unmeasured benefits to consumers. As mentioned, the services yielded by consumer capital stocks could be part of a differently defined set of national accounts. If the definitions were changed, consumer expenditures on durable goods would be a form of investment; on that basis, to arrive at a flow of services from the consumer durable stock, depreciation and a rate of return on this capital would have to be imputed. According to current U.S. definitions, similar estimates have long been made for owner-occupied housing. Extending this treatment to consumer durables would yield results superior to the present treatment in the U.S. national accounts.

PERCENTAGE DISTRIBUTION OF U.S. NET FIXED CAPITAL STOCK, BY OWNERSHIP, 1959–1997

BASED ON STOCKS IN CHAINED 1992 DOLLARS

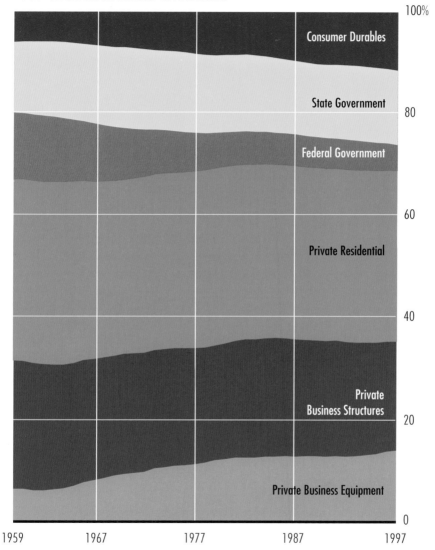

Government capital is often excluded in analyzing the growth of private business output. Its contribution to the growth of output and productivity remains controversial.

There is no denying that government investments yield benefits—such as the increased speed and ease that individuals enjoy when traveling over our modern highway system. Benefits of this sort, however, are excluded from GDP. The practical question arises in this connection with measured output: How much does government investment contribute to the long-term growth of productivity in the private business sector?

Those who believe that the contribution is large cite the slow growth of public infrastructure as an important factor in the slower growth of business productivity since the early 1970s. Critics, however, have questioned the validity of this evidence. They concede that infrastructure such as the interstate highway system has reduced business costs to some extent, but they remain skeptics, citing the difficulties in measuring both benefits and costs. Government investment is not subject to the discipline of the market. For example, benefits from the public infrastructure as great as its proponents claim imply a huge rate of return on government capital. If that is so, critics ask, why doesn't the public demand big new programs for public construction to be financed by higher taxes or new bond issues?

Other critics have raised a question regarding causation: Does reduced infrastructure investment cause slower growth, or does slower growth of the economy result in reduced spending on infrastructure?

If nothing else, potholes remind us that we need public investment and that a large, rich country needs a lot of it. But with our present knowledge, economists cannot pinpoint the exact importance of public investment as an influence on productivity growth in private business.

NET CAPITAL STOCKS OWNED BY GOVERNMENTS, 1959–1997

TRILLIONS OF CHAINED 1992 DOLLARS

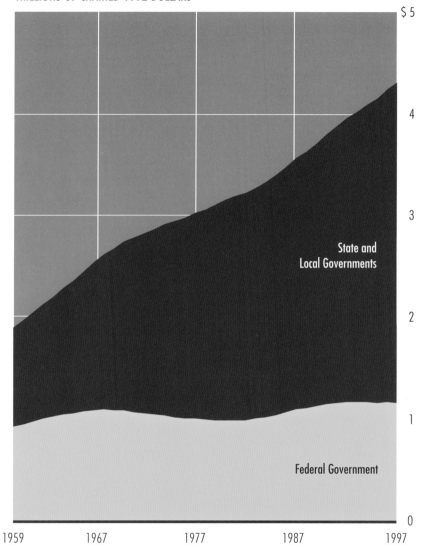

State and
Local Governments

Federal Government

$ 5

4

3

2

1

0

1959   1967   1977   1987   1997

Expenditures for research and development have expanded our scientific and technological knowledge, which has contributed to the rise in productivity.

Recent studies of growth have increasingly included intangible capital. Human capital was touched on earlier. Another form of intangible capital is the "stock" of scientific and technological knowledge. Some of it is a consequence of scientific advances and great inventions, such as the steam engine and the computer. Economists believe that much of it is a result of research and development expenditures by business, government, and universities. The chart, based on estimates from the Bureau of Labor Statistics, shows R&D net stocks of nonfarm business in 1992 dollars and the corresponding net stocks of tangible capital.

Research affects productivity growth of the private economy as a whole because of its spillover effects, or what economists call *externalities*. Much basic research—as distinct from applied research—is of this nature, because the findings of basic research are typically published in a scientific journal and are available to all, rather than to a particular firm or researcher, although the patent system allows an inventor to profit from a technological breakthrough.

Although the availability of time series on R&D expenditures has encouraged the development of estimates of the stock of research and development capital, many estimating problems remain. For example, the unit of research activity is hard to define. We lack market prices for much of the stock. How much of R&D is intermediate output, that is, research undertaken simply to carry out a customer's order? How do we distinguish routine research from what turns out to be an important breakthrough? Economists have found long lags between the time of an invention or its first practical application, on the one hand, and productivity change, on the other. This reflects the fact that the learning process takes time.

A common view is that R&D is important as a source of productivity change for the private business economy as a whole—but just how important cannot be determined easily. R&D probably contributes more than the relatively small contribution that can be measured with a fair degree of certainty.

NET STOCK OF R&D CAPITAL COMPARED WITH PRODUCTIVE CAPITAL STOCKS OF PRIVATE NONFARM BUSINESS, 1948–1996

BILLIONS OF 1992 DOLLARS, LOGARITHMIC SCALE

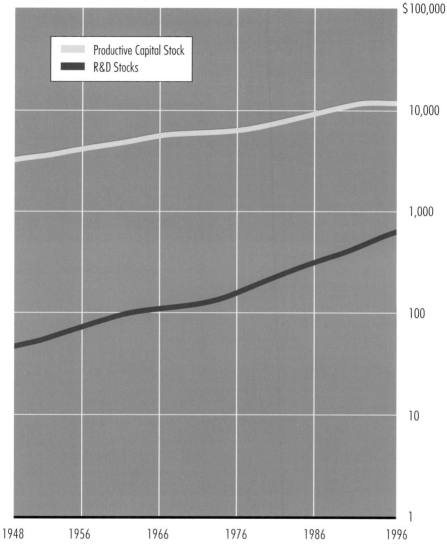

Natural resources are part of the nation's capital. Estimating these stocks poses many difficulties.

The treatment of natural resources in our national economic accounts is not satisfactory. Important aspects of natural resources are ignored. Suppose that a mineral deposit that existed at the start of a period is exhausted at the end. Whatever income was generated by the mining activity has been overstated if the exhaustion of the resource has not been accounted for. Similarly, if the exploration results in a discovery, the value of the new deposit should be counted as an addition to wealth, but at present it is not.

This treatment of natural resources differs from the way "reproducible" capital, such as structures and equipment, is treated. Capital that has a long life is depreciated as it is used up, just as capital stocks are augmented when new private investment in plant and equipment is undertaken. Estimating difficulties help explain the slow statistical progress. The future yield of new discoveries is uncertain. In the 1940s and 1950s, it was common to see statements that the United States would "run out of oil" in a certain number of years. It is not easy to account for the loss of value that occurs as a resource is used up. Estimating the current value of a natural resource requires estimates of interest rates and rents, often far into the future. A comprehensive set of market prices for the natural resource might solve the calculation problems, but the price information is inadequate. In any case, such prices as exist reflect a return both on invested capital in the form of plant and equipment and on the resource in the ground. The problem is to disentangle the two.

Early in 1994, the Commerce Department took steps (since discontinued) to set up "satellite" accounts for natural resources. Reflecting the many uncertainties, Commerce made four different estimates of end-of-year stocks of all mineral resources (dominated by petroleum) in the United States from 1958 to 1991. The range of estimates illustrated in the chart is quite large, but the figures can at least be seen as part of the existing broad system of national accounts. These natural resource stocks are large: roughly $0.5–1 trillion, or 3–7 percent of the stock of reproducible capital, at the end of 1991. In real terms, these stocks are almost unchanged from 1958 to 1991. When these natural resources are accounted for, the return on all private capital, being spread over a larger base, is somewhat lower than had been thought.

STOCKS OF SUBSOIL ASSETS BY VALUATION METHOD, 1958–1991

TRILLIONS OF 1987 DOLLARS

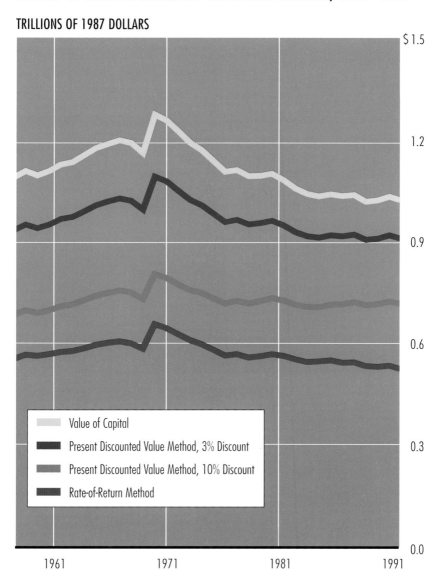

	Value of Capital		
	Present Discounted Value Method, 3% Discount		
	Present Discounted Value Method, 10% Discount		
	Rate-of-Return Method		

Economists disagree about why the nation's output has risen faster than the combined inputs of labor and capital.

Although most investigators have found that, over the postwar period as a whole, productivity change accounts for a significant part of the rise in output, economists do not have satisfactory answers to explain what lies behind the growth in productivity. The standard answer is "improved technology" or "technical progress." Although this interpretation is undoubtedly correct, economists have found the answer inadequate because it is too inclusive and cannot itself be measured well.

The chart illustrates some findings by the Bureau of Labor Statistics for the private economy, starting with the rise of 2.3 percent per year in output per hour of labor from 1948 to 1997. The contribution of increased capital intensity—capital services per hour of labor—is 0.8 percent per year. The BLS also makes an allowance of 0.2 percent a year for the improved quality of labor (the combined influences of education, work experience, and gender). The output rise of 2.3 percent minus the effects of increased capital intensity (0.8) and improved labor quality (0.2) leaves a rise of 1.3 percent (rounded) in multifactor productivity. This number is more than half the total rise in the rate of growth in output per hour.

The BLS also estimated the influence of R&D for the nonfarm sector, which yielded a contribution of 0.2 percent per year. Putting aside the qualifications regarding R&D mentioned earlier, and assuming this contribution of 0.2 percent was the same in the entire business sector including farms, we are still left with 1.1 percentage points unexplained (1.3 – 0.2).

Edward Denison emphasized the movement of resources off farms and out of small businesses, where they cannot be used efficiently, into larger-scale nonfarm activities. He also stressed the importance of the economies of large-scale production and marketing. His figures, however, were essentially judgmental, rather than hard estimates. Many other influences have been investigated, but either they have not been important or they have lacked a solid factual basis. Taking account of measured influences still leaves a large unexplained residual, variously called *technical progress* or *advances in knowledge.*

In view of these results, a remark made by Moses Abramovitz many years ago seems appropriate. He said that the inability of economists to measure what lies behind productivity growth is a measure of economists' ignorance.

CONTRIBUTION TO CHANGE IN OUTPUT
PER HOUR OF LABOR, 1948–1997

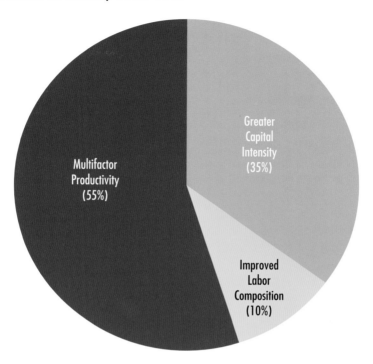

Greater
Capital
Intensity
(35%)

Multifactor
Productivity
(55%)

Improved
Labor
Composition
(10%)

Relative to GDP, the amount of domestic saving available to finance private investment declined in the 1980s and 1990s until 1997, when it turned up.

Capital stocks are the accumulation of investment flows, whose financing depends on savings. Total savings for the nation embrace not only private savings but also government savings and foreign savings invested here (the *capital inflow*, shown on page 73).

Private savings as a percentage of GDP were fairly stable in the first three decades shown here and declined only in the 1990s. Total savings declined in each period before 1997, however, because government savings were declining. *Government savings* are defined here as the excess of government revenues over expenditures, excluding investment expenditures but including depreciation as an expenditure. (These savings thus differ from the *conventional surplus*, which is the excess of revenues over expenditures, including investment expenditures but not including depreciation as an expenditure.) In all periods shown here, government savings, though declining, were positive. Federal savings were negative but were offset by the savings of state and local governments. The total of government savings, however, was less than the total of government investment: governments drew on private savings to finance their investments. For example, in the 1970s, government savings were 2.6 percent of GDP, but government investment was 3.6 percent of GDP. This difference absorbed an amount of private savings equal to 1 percent of GDP. As a result, although private savings equaled 17.2 percent of GDP, only 16.2 percent was available to finance private investment.

The absorption of private savings to finance government investment increased up to 1997. Thus, the savings available to finance private investment fell substantially, from 16.2 percent of GDP in the 1960s to 12.4 percent in 1990–1996.

The picture became considerably different in 1997 and 1998, when the federal government began to generate positive savings. Then, total government savings exceeded government investment and, instead of absorbing private savings, government became a provider of savings to finance private investment.

U.S GROSS SAVING AS PERCENTAGE OF GDP, 1960–1998

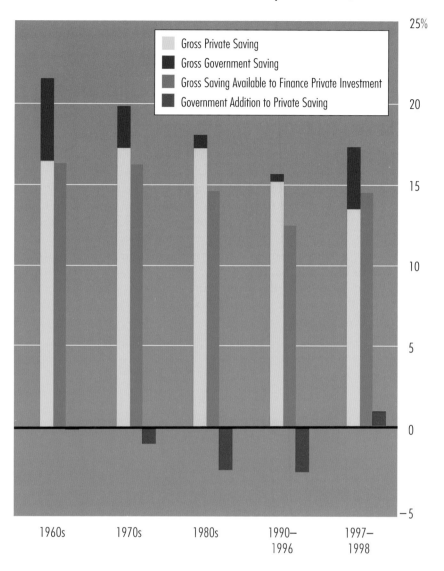

Gross Private Saving
Gross Government Saving
Gross Saving Available to Finance Private Investment
Government Addition to Private Saving

1960s   1970s   1980s   1990–   1997–
                        1996   1998

In the 1990s, investment in the United States declined, relative to GDP, as domestic saving and the capital inflow both declined.

In the first three decades shown here, total domestic investment, private plus government, remained near 20 percent of GDP, despite a decline of domestic saving. The decline of domestic saving was largely offset by the change in the international flow of capital. In the 1960s and 1970s, capital flowed out of the United States to be invested abroad. In the 1980s, however, capital flowed into the United States. From the 1960s to the 1980s, the shift in the capital flow was equal to 2.2 percent of GDP, compared with a decline of 3.6 percent in the domestic saving rate. In the 1990s, until 1997, however, the capital inflow was lower, while the domestic saving rate also declined. Domestic investment fell to 17 percent of GDP.

This combination of events does not necessarily mean that investment was lower in the 1990s because the capital inflow was lower. Causation may have run in the other direction. If investment opportunities here had been greater—relative to opportunities elsewhere—the capital inflow might have been greater.

U.S. SAVING AND INVESTMENT AS PERCENTAGE OF GDP, DECADE AVERAGES, 1960–1998

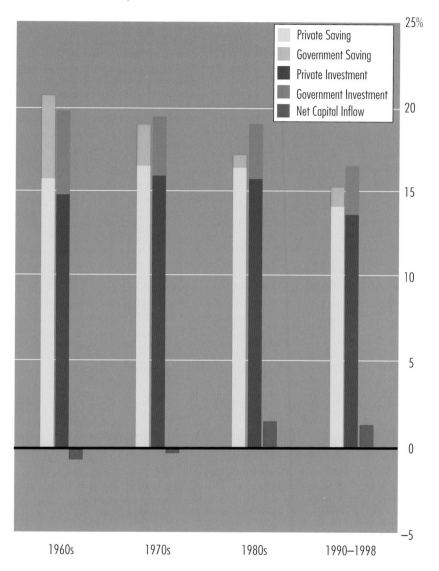

Legend:
- Private Saving
- Government Saving
- Private Investment
- Government Investment
- Net Capital Inflow

1960s   1970s   1980s   1990–1998

Personal saving has declined since the early 1980s.

Gross private saving is made up of saving by households—personal saving—and saving by businesses. From the 1950s to the 1970s, personal saving constituted about one-third of the gross private total, but it fell in the mid-1980s and 1990s and reached about 2–3 percent in 1998. Personal saving is usually discussed in relation to personal disposable (after-tax) income, as illustrated in the top chart. That rate reached a high point of 9.4 percent in 1981 and fell irregularly to less than 1 percent in 1998.

The saving statistics pose many measurement difficulties. Personal saving is the difference between two large aggregates, income and consumption. Any errors in estimating these aggregates will show up in the personal saving residual—hence the irregular behavior of the saving rate. A common explanation of the steep decline in the personal saving rate since the 1980s is the extraordinary rise in the stock market. Because investment in the national accounts measures only real additions to wealth—more buildings, more equipment, and so forth—all types of capital gains reflecting pure price increases on the assets that individuals own, or gains on the sale of assets, are excluded from income and thus from personal saving. However, capital gains on individuals' stock holdings, in their portfolios or pensions, are causing consumer balance sheets to balloon and are thought by many economists to be a major influence in the strong increases in real consumer spending. (See page 76 and part eleven.)

Saving by corporations consists of (1) retained earnings, or what corporations plow back after paying dividends and income taxes, and (2) the funds set aside for depreciation. Depreciation is, by far, the biggest component of gross private saving. The picture for unincorporated businesses is the same as for corporations, except that it also embraces an annual depreciation allowance on the entire U.S. stock of owner-occupied homes.

Many economists prefer to measure national saving on a net basis rather than on a gross basis, that is, exclusive of depreciation, for the same reason that they prefer to measure production by the net product rather than by the gross product. In this view, the relative stability of the gross saving ratio is misleading, because it hides the fact that, since the 1960s, depreciation has risen relative to output while the ratio of net saving to output has declined. Not much is known about economic depreciation—how different kinds of business equipment and buildings lose value because of wear and tear and because of the appearance of superior capital goods that make the use of older capital uneconomic.

PERSONAL SAVING AS PERCENTAGE OF DISPOSABLE PERSONAL INCOME, 1947–1998

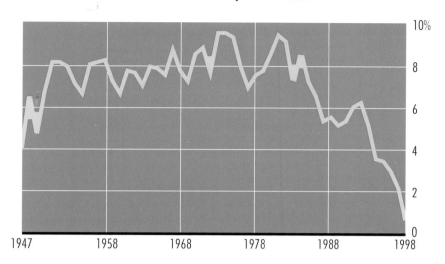

GROSS PRIVATE SAVING, NET SAVING, AND DEPRECIATION AS PERCENTAGES OF GDP, 1950–1998

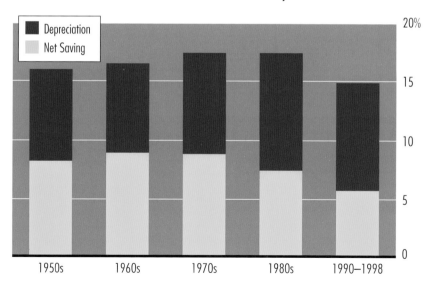

The chart shows, for the years 1987–1996, the average percentage of GDP saved in the United States and other countries, by the definition of *saving* that most countries have adopted for their national accounts. *Saving* is defined as GDP less consumption, with *consumption* defined to include not only personal consumption but also government consumption. In this definition, government expenditures for research and development, for education, and for defense are considered consumption, except where the expenditures are for structures and durable equipment. Consumer expenditures for consumer durable goods are also considered consumption. A definition of *saving* that included all these items as investment and saving would probably bring the U.S. ratio up to the level of Italy and possibly to the level of France, but still leave it below that of Germany and Japan. We do not, however, have reliable standardized figures to verify that.

The foregoing observations relate to total savings, private and governmental. There is little doubt that the private savings rate is lower in the United States than in the other industrial countries. Most items that would be included in a broader definition of saving would be in the government sector. Also, the division between private and public savings is partly a matter of accounting. Funds accumulated in a government fund to pay retirement benefits would be considered public, not private, savings, whereas they would be considered private savings if accumulated in private funds.

Still, there are real differences in national savings levels, no matter how they are defined. The relatively low level of savings in the United States, at least as compared with Japan and Germany, is sometimes attributed to the high level of per capita wealth in this country.

GROSS SAVING AS PERCENTAGE OF GDP
BY COUNTRY, 1987–1996 AVERAGE

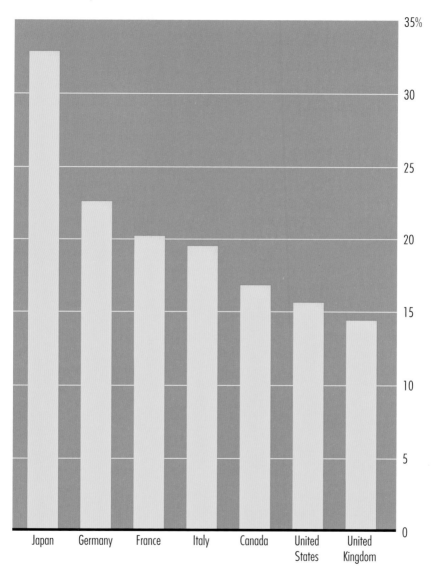

The rate of productivity growth has not been constant. The slowdown after 1973, in the United States and other countries, is not well understood.

Although output per hour of labor in the business sector grew 2.3 percent from 1948 to 1997, the growth has not been constant. The rate was 3.3 percent from 1948 to 1972, but only 1.3 percent from 1973 to 1997, according to the Bureau of Labor Statistics. The slowdown is evident whether productivity is measured by output per hour of labor (top chart) or per unit of all inputs combined. Over the past decade or so, moreover, slower rates of productivity growth appear in all leading industrial countries.

Not only has the rate of productivity growth slowed down, but its importance in output growth appears to have diminished. This is illustrated in the pie charts on page 79, which decompose the growth rate of output per hour into the contribution of greater capital intensity, of improved labor composition, and of multifactor productivity. From 1948 to 1972, multifactor productivity growth was a large fraction—64 percent—of the growth of output per labor hour. From 1972 to 1997, productivity growth was only 34 percent of the much smaller growth in output per labor hour.

Since the late 1970s, the slowdown in the rate of productivity growth has been the subject of much research and intense speculation, but no consensus has emerged about the causes. Some economists ask whether it is valid to employ as a standard of comparison the first two decades or so after World War II, when demand was abnormally high. In recent years, questions have arisen about the pace of technological change, particularly about whether its character has changed or is being changed. Downgrading the importance of multifactor productivity change in accounting for output change is a new aspect of the problem and has only added to the puzzle.

Investigators in this field have been paying increasing attention to the data that underlie the productivity calculations. For example, although economists can make a good case for some upward bias in the calculation of price change from the 1980s to the 1990s, demonstrating a slowdown in productivity growth from that source requires showing that the bias has worsened as compared with the past. Unfortunately, the lack of data virtually prevents a solid reconstruction of the historical record.

OUTPUT PER HOUR OF LABOR—PERCENTAGE CHANGE FROM PRECEDING YEAR, 1949–1997

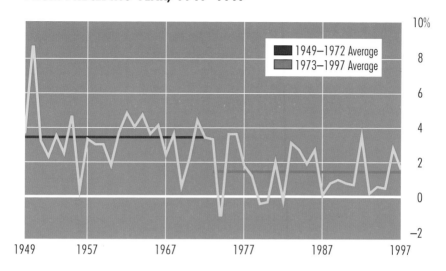

1949–1972 Average
1973–1997 Average

10%
8
6
4
2
0
−2

1949   1957   1967   1977   1987   1997

CONTRIBUTION TO CHANGE IN OUTPUT PER HOUR OF LABOR

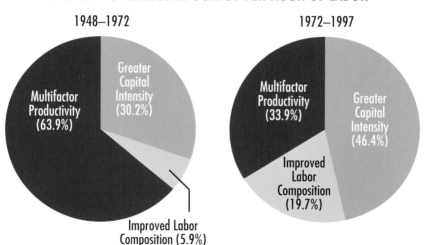

1948–1972

Multifactor Productivity (63.9%)
Greater Capital Intensity (30.2%)
Improved Labor Composition (5.9%)

1972–1997

Multifactor Productivity (33.9%)
Greater Capital Intensity (46.4%)
Improved Labor Composition (19.7%)

Since the early 1970s, growth in the amount of capital available to labor has also slowed slightly, but not nearly as much as output per hour of labor.

One argument about the decline in productivity growth emphasizes the low rate of investment in this country. This view attributes the decline in saving over the past decade mainly to the large budget deficits of the federal government that continued through 1997. Since the capital stock grows through additions of investment and since investment depends on saving, a reduced saving rate means a reduced rate of increase in the stock of capital available for labor. (The stock of capital refers to the buildings, equipment, land, and inventories available to workers in private business.)

One problem with this argument is that the rate of growth of the capital stock did not slow down much. This country experienced large inflows of capital from abroad, which compensated for the low rate of national saving.

The relevant figures for analyzing this issue are output per labor hour and capital per labor hour, which are shown in the chart. The growth in capital per hour fell from an average annual rate of 3.1 percent (1948–1973) to 2.0 percent (1973–1997). Since capital has a weight of about 30 percent in this kind of accounting, it cannot explain much of the decline in labor productivity. Output per labor hour fell from a rate of 3.3 percent over the period 1948–1973 to 1.3 percent over the period 1973–1997.

Capital per worker is indeed important, as explained. But its growth is far from being the complete explanation of labor productivity growth or of the slowdown in that growth.

OUTPUT AND CAPITAL PER HOUR OF LABOR
IN PRIVATE BUSINESS, 1948–1997

INDEXES: 1948=100

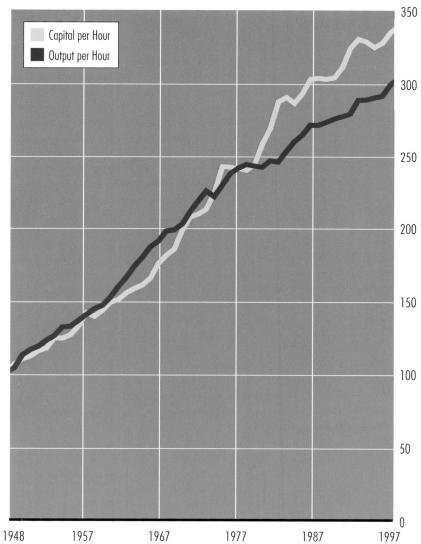

PART SIX

Labor Force and Employment

The proportion of all working-aged women who are in the work force has increased, while the corresponding proportion of working-aged men has decreased.

Since World War II, strong employment growth has been accompanied by a decline in the length of the workweek. Since 1948, the number of jobs has risen by 125 percent. The desire of people to seek work and their ability to find work have outstripped the rise in the working-age population. About 22 percent of the labor force increase from 1948 to 1998 represents an increase in the proportion of the population (sixteen years and older) in the labor force.

The civilian participation rate in the labor force, or the ratio of the number of persons in the labor force to the number of persons sixteen years and older, has been rising almost steadily through the postwar period. Increases among women have been large and persistent, more than offsetting decreases among men. For men sixty-five years and older, participation rates fell from 46 percent in 1950 to 17 percent in 1998. For men between the ages of fifty-five and sixty-four, participation rates fell from 87 percent to 68 percent over the same period.

Changes in participation rates have been influenced by several long-run factors. For men, the greater availability and size of pension benefits, both public and private, have led them to retire earlier. For women, changed attitudes toward participation in the labor force and toward the age of marriage and childbearing—and the civil rights legislation of the mid-1960s—in a setting of rising labor demand have been important.

Changes in rates of participation in the labor force in this country, though not unique, are not universal. Among the large countries of the Organization for Economic Cooperation and Development, Canada has had an experience similar to ours; the experience of the United Kingdom has been somewhat similar, but with less-pronounced change. Japan, Germany, France, and Italy have experienced decreases in total civilian participation rates since the 1960s.

At present, civilian labor force participation rates in Canada, Japan, and the United Kingdom are either close to or slightly below those in this country. Rates are considerably lower, however, in Germany, France, and especially Italy, where both men and women of working age are less likely to be in the labor force.

PARTICIPATION IN THE LABOR FORCE BY MALES AND FEMALES, 1948–1998

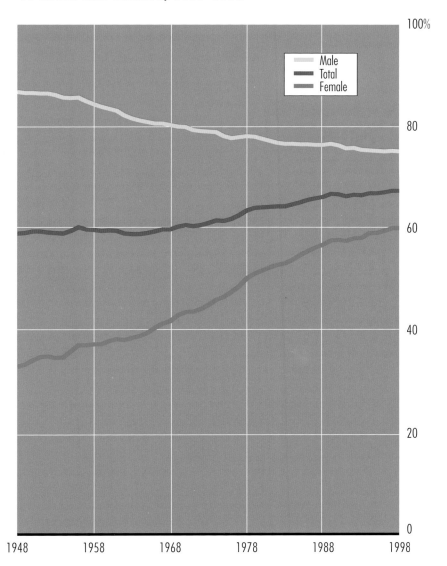

Note: Based on calculations of civilian labor force as percentages of population sixteen years and older in each group.

The charts on page 87 show rates of labor force participation by educational attainment, separately for men and women, for persons between the ages of twenty-five and sixty-four. The data are available only since 1970.

In 1970, participation rates among men showed only slight variation by educational attainment. Men without a high school diploma had an 89 percent participation rate, while each of the three other groups had a rate of 96 percent. The picture was quite different in 1998. Each group had a lower rate than in 1970, but the decline was small for the two groups with the most education and was pronounced for those who did not graduate from high school (top chart).

In 1970, participation rates for women varied directly with educational attainment: the rate for women with a college degree was 42 percent greater than for women who did not graduate from high school. This pattern changed greatly by 1998. In contrast to the male experience, participation rates for all women's groups rose, but as with the men, participation rates became much more dispersed. The smallest rise occurred among the least educated despite some acceleration in 1997 and 1998. The 1998 participation rate for women with a college degree was 66 percent greater than the rate for women without a high school diploma (bottom chart).

If the greater size and availability of pensions—public and private—are the chief reasons for declining participation rates among men, what accounts for the differential by educational attainment? Prospects for advancement must be an important factor. Persons with little education reach their peak earning power earlier in life than persons with a college degree or more. Unemployment rates are highest for the least educated. Low participation rates for the least educated may also be attributable to the nature of their work. Their jobs are likely to be physically demanding and uninteresting, and persons holding such jobs may welcome release from the work. Acquiring more education as a means of getting a higher-paying job may be a feasible option for a young person, but not for a person in middle age. Thus, the labor market and the nature of the work can make retirement a relatively superior alternative for the least skilled.

LABOR FORCE PARTICIPATION RATES OF MEN TWENTY-FIVE TO SIXTY-FOUR, BY EDUCATIONAL ATTAINMENT, 1970–1998

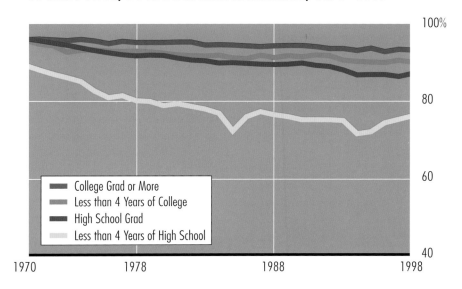

College Grad or More
Less than 4 Years of College
High School Grad
Less than 4 Years of High School

LABOR FORCE PARTICIPATION RATES OF WOMEN TWENTY-FIVE TO SIXTY-FOUR, BY EDUCATIONAL ATTAINMENT, 1970–1998

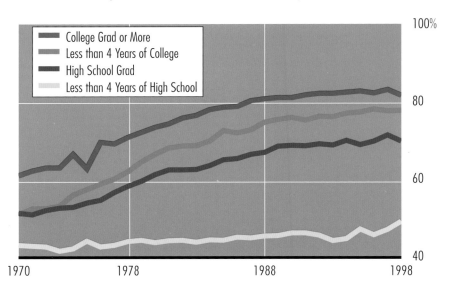

College Grad or More
Less than 4 Years of College
High School Grad
Less than 4 Years of High School

Employment increases at different rates in different industries, and even in a period when total employment is increasing, employment in some industries is declining.

From 1987 to 1997, total employment in private industries increased by 20 percent. In that period, however, employment declined in industries that in 1987 had accounted for 16 percent of total employment. (These calculations are based on a division of total employment among sixty-five industries. If they were based on a finer division of industries, the dispersion would be greater.) Employment declined by 40 percent in coal mining, by 25 percent in the production of apparel and other textile products, and by 20 percent in private households. In contrast, employment increased by 86 percent in business services and by 43 percent in health services. These two industries accounted for 13 percent of total employment in 1987 and 37 percent of the increase to 1997.

Still, a large proportion of all employment was concentrated in industries that experienced an average increase. In 1987, 42 percent of all workers labored in industries recording 10–30 percent increases by 1997.

Three main factors explain the differences in employment experience in different industries: changes in the pattern of demand, differences in productivity growth, and differences in the impact of foreign trade. The most striking aspect is the clear ability of the economy to adapt to great changes in demand, productivity, and foreign competition—which affect different industries differently—and still to maintain high employment growth and relatively low unemployment.

DISTRIBUTION OF WORKERS BY PERCENTAGE CHANGE
IN EMPLOYMENT IN THEIR INDUSTRIES, 1987–1997

PERCENT OF WORKERS

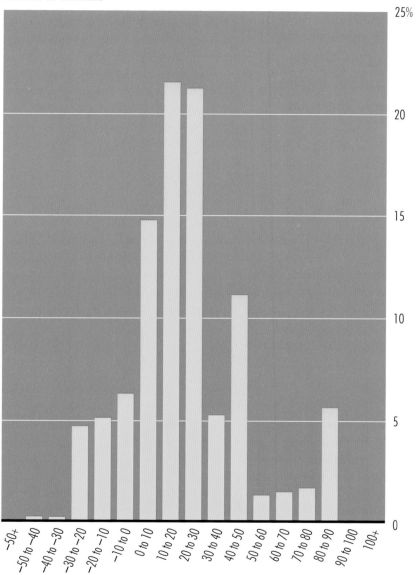

PERCENTAGE INCREASE OR DECREASE IN INDUSTRY EMPLOYMENT

As the industrial composition of jobs has changed, blue-collar jobs have declined in importance, and white-collar jobs have become more important.

Employment in the United States not only has risen considerably over the postwar period but also has undergone a substantial change in character. In 1948, industrial employment (manufacturing, mining, and construction) accounted for 48 percent of all wage and salary workers in the nonfarm sector. In 1998, industrial employment was one-third higher than in 1948, but the rise in employment in the rest of the private economy was much faster, so that the industrial share was only 24 percent. The major OECD countries experienced absolute declines in industrial employment over the postwar years.

The slower growth in U.S. industrial employment reflected shifts in industry demands and—despite problems with data—a more rapid rise in labor productivity in industry than elsewhere in the private economy. Labor productivity rose as manufacturers and mining companies substituted capital for labor, especially on the factory floor. Changing technology put more emphasis on jobs in the office than on jobs in the plant.

One result of these developments shows up in the changing relative importance of blue- and white-collar jobs. In 1958, blue-collar jobs accounted for 37 percent of total U.S. employment; in 1998, 25 percent. Over the same period, the share of white-collar jobs rose from 43 to 59 percent. The importance of blue-collar jobs declined among both men and women, but the decline among women was especially large. Although women are now found in occupations once the exclusive province of men, women have a strong preference for white-collar work.

White-collar workers can be divided into two main groups. During the 1990s, the rise in the relative importance of white-collar workers has been concentrated in the group of occupations ordinarily requiring college and graduate work, such as managers and professional specialists. Since the recession of 1990–1991, employment in the other group—consisting of salespersons, office workers, and technicians—has risen, but its share of total employment has declined.

The chart does not show two other categories of workers: farm workers, almost all of whom are blue-collar and whose importance has declined sharply over the years, and "service workers," a mixed group whose general importance has increased slightly.

EMPLOYMENT IN BLUE- AND WHITE-COLLAR OCCUPATIONS AS PERCENTAGES OF TOTAL EMPLOYMENT, 1958–1998

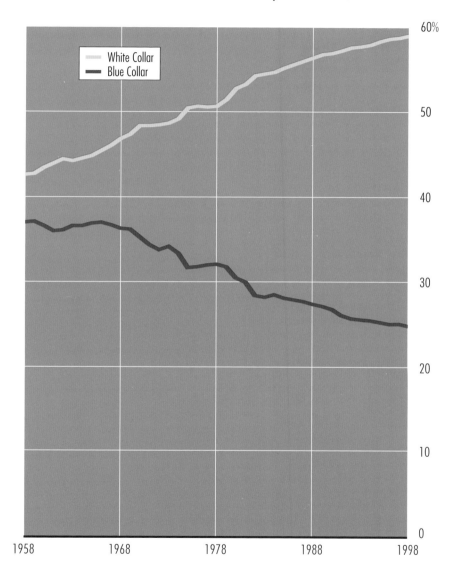

Agricultural employment as a share of total employment has fallen sharply in the United States, and much more in other industrialized countries.

Employment in agriculture in the United States was 8 percent of civilian employment in 1960 and only 2.8 percent in 1997. Declining farm employment in this country was part of a worldwide phenomenon. Over the same period, for example, all major countries of the Organization for Economic Cooperation and Development experienced employment decreases in agriculture. In none of those countries today is agricultural employment as much as 10 percent of the total.

Most surprising is how large these ratios were in other countries in 1960. In that year, agriculture was more than 30 percent of total civilian employment in Italy, 30 percent in Japan, and 23 percent in France. One would have to go back to 1910 to find a ratio that high in the United States. As in this country, the movement of resources out of agriculture to industry was an important factor in the productivity rise in Western Europe, Canada, and Japan over this period. In most of those countries, however, agricultural employment is now so low that this source of productivity increase is largely spent.

AGRICULTURAL EMPLOYMENT AS PERCENTAGE OF CIVILIAN EMPLOYMENT FOR SELECTED COUNTRIES, 1960 AND 1997

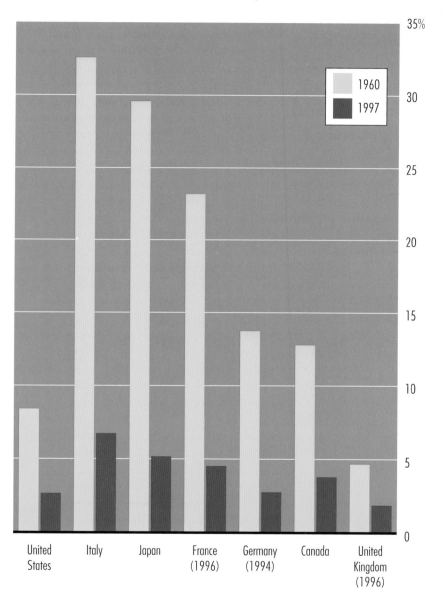

The work year has become shorter. About 7 percent of the hours for which an employee is paid represents paid vacations or other paid leave.

The long-term continuous decline in the length of the average workweek and work year since the second half of the nineteenth century has lasted through the post–World War II era. The postwar decrease has reflected a shorter workweek for full-time workers as well as a large increase in the proportion of workers employed part-time.

The lower line of the chart traces the course of average annual hours, obtained by dividing total hours by the sum of full-time and part-time employees in private nonfarm industries. The upper line divides the same aggregate hours by the number of full-time equivalent employees. (Two workers, each of whom worked half a full-time week, are considered the equivalent of one full-time worker. Full-time work schedules may vary by industry.) The difference between the two lines shows how the increased proportion of part-time workers in total employment has affected hours. For full-time equivalent workers, the average annual rate of decrease in hours from 1948 to 1997—0.13 percent—is much less than the annual average decline of about 0.5 percent in the first half of the twentieth century (from 1909 to 1947).

The rise in part-time employment has been large. In 1968, persons usually working part time (typically, less than thirty-five hours a week) were 14 percent of employed persons. In 1998, that proportion had risen to 18 percent. Part-time work becomes more prevalent during recessions, but typically, and especially in high-employment years, most persons with part-time jobs work a shorter week voluntarily. In 1998, persons working short hours because of slack conditions or because they could find only part-time jobs were only 13 percent of all persons working fewer than thirty-five hours a week.

All figures just discussed are based on the number of hours in a year for which an employee is on the job. The Bureau of Labor Statistics estimates that, in 1997, production workers and nonsupervisory employees in nonfarm business actually worked 93.4 percent of the number of hours for which they were paid. The difference represents paid vacations, holidays, and personal and administrative leave, such as jury duty. For a full-time year-round job in nonfarm industries, 7 percent represents three and a half weeks of paid leave, or a two-week vacation plus several additional days, on the basis of a full-time 1997 work year of about 1,900 hours.

AVERAGE ANNUAL HOURS PER EMPLOYEE
IN PRIVATE NONFARM INDUSTRIES, 1948–1997

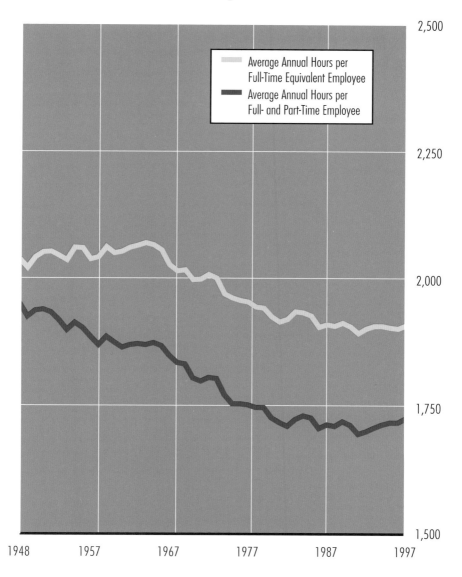

Average Annual Hours per Full-Time Equivalent Employee

Average Annual Hours per Full- and Part-Time Employee

2,500

2,250

2,000

1,750

1,500

1948   1957   1967   1977   1987   1997

Increased longevity and a shorter working life have lengthened the period of retirement for men.

A baby born in 1900 had a life expectancy of only 47.0 years. A baby born in 1997 had a life expectancy of 76.2 years. These figures for the United States, while high, are by no means the highest in the world. Sixteen other countries had figures as high or higher, with Japan in the lead for large industrialized countries at 79.7 years.

At the beginning of this century, a man of 20 could expect to live an additional 42 years, during which he could expect to work 38 years. The period of retirement was thus brief. As of 1997, life expectancy for an average 20-year-old man had risen by 12 years, while his expected working life was lower by about 2 years. With a longer life expectancy and a shorter working life, the expected span of retirement rose to 18 years, up from 4 years at the turn of the century. Put another way, in 1900, a man of 20 could expect to work 90 percent of his remaining life; 90 years later, that proportion had fallen to 68 percent.

Life expectancy for women has risen even more than for men over this period—from 44 to 60 years for a woman of 20. Working-life figures for women have also risen, as women's participation in the labor force has gone up. In 1900, a woman of 20 could expect to be actively working in paid employment for only 14 percent of her life; by 1990, that share was approximately 50 percent. The average for the early period reflects a small proportion of women with work experience and a large proportion with none at all or very little.

Estimates of working-life expectancies for the late 1990s are not available. If they were, they would probably show a small decline for males and some increase for females since 1990. Coupled with rising life expectancies, these trends imply more leisure for men—but probably not for women.

LIFE AND WORKING-LIFE EXPECTANCIES
FOR MALES AGED TWENTY YEARS, 1900–1997

NUMBER OF ADDITIONAL YEARS

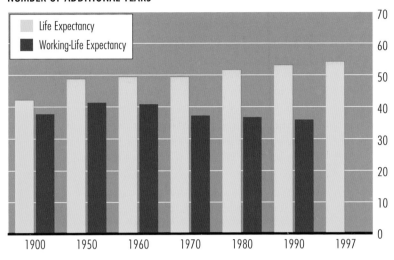

LIFE AND WORKING-LIFE EXPECTANCIES
FOR FEMALES AGED TWENTY YEARS, 1900–1997

NUMBER OF ADDITIONAL YEARS

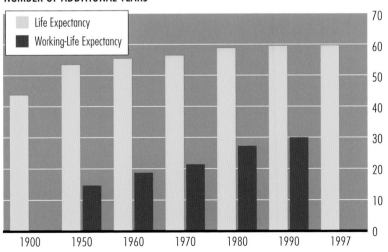

Note: Working-life expectancies not available for 1997 or for females in 1900.

Participation rates of black male teenagers in the labor force have fallen, as rates of black female teenagers have risen.

Although black adult men have made genuine progress in entering the labor force and finding jobs over the postwar period, that is not true of black male teenagers. Their position in the labor force has deteriorated and is a serious problem for society.

In 1966–1968, participation in the labor force by black and other males aged sixteen to nineteen was a little lower than by white males of the same age. Thirty years later, the rate of white male teenagers was a little higher than before, while the corresponding rate of blacks had fallen and was only two-thirds of the white rate. The behavior of black males contrasts with the behavior of black female teenagers, whose participation rates increased over the period, although not as much as of white female teenagers.

The participation rates of both black and white adult males (aged twenty and older) fell over the period. In 1966–1968, the rate of black male teenagers was 62 percent of the rate for black male adults. Thirty years later, that proportion had fallen to 54 percent. Increased school enrollment might account for some decline in labor force participation of black male teenagers from the 1960s to 1996–1998. Over the same period, however, increased school enrollment among black female teenagers did not stand in the way of increased participation in the labor force.

PERCENTAGE OF MALES AGED SIXTEEN TO NINETEEN IN THE CIVILIAN LABOR FORCE, 1966–1998

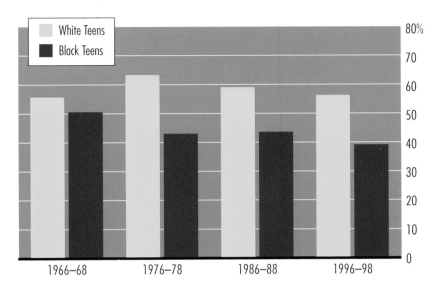

PERCENTAGE OF FEMALES AGED SIXTEEN TO NINETEEN IN THE CIVILIAN LABOR FORCE, 1966–1998

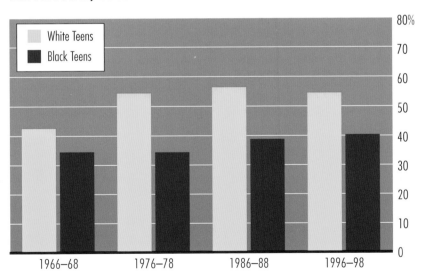

Population growth in this country has slowed since the earlier post–World War II years. The changing distribution by age points to many problems in the twenty-first century.

For public policy, the most important issue raised by the changing age distribution concerns the long-term viability of our Social Security system. The main question is whether there will be a sufficient number of persons of working age in the twenty-first century to support the very large increase in retirees. Given existing provisions for benefits and taxes under our Social Security system, the answer appears uncertain; that is why the issue was being actively debated toward the end of the twentieth century.

The Social Security Administration calculates a statistic called the *aged-dependency ratio*, which is the number of persons from age twenty to sixty-four (the approximate working population) relative to the number who are sixty-five years and older. That statistic fell from 5.78 in 1960 to 4.78 in 1990 and is expected to fall to 3.64 in 2020 (see the chart). The pronounced decline from 1990 to 2020 would reflect, on the one hand, the expected slowdown in the growth of the labor force and, on the other, the reaching of retirement age by the above-average baby-boom cohorts born in the first two decades after the end of World War II. The same population distribution has implications for Medicare, which is an entitlement of almost all persons reaching age sixty-five.

In a variety of ways, businesses adapt to changing age distributions as they affect the demand for products, supplies of labor, and costs. Also, workers respond to changing incentives provided by new legislation. For example, earlier in the postwar period, private pension benefits tended to be "defined benefit" plans—so many dollars per year for the retiree. From an actuarial point of view, those benefits were based on the assumption that the age distribution of employees would remain relatively youthful. In time, however, that assumption became less and less tenable, so private businesses began to switch to "defined contribution" plans. Under that arrangement, the worker has a certain percentage taken from his paycheck, but the employer is under no obligation to pay any specific amount at retirement. Even so, workers have shown a preference for these plans, because they themselves, as they learn more about investment, make their own decisions regarding risks and returns in their pension portfolios.

RATIO OF WORKING-AGE AMERICANS (TWENTY TO SIXTY-FOUR) TO OLDER AMERICANS (SIXTY-FIVE AND OLDER), 1960–2075

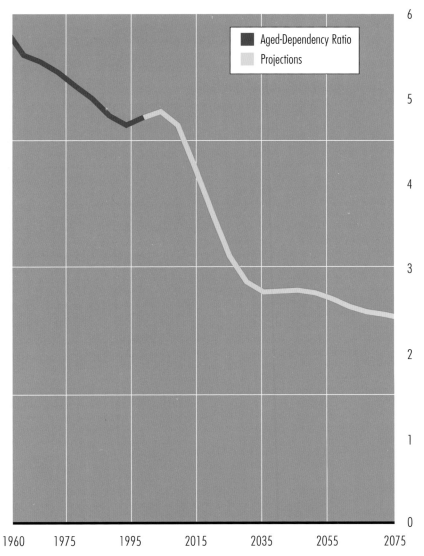

Note: Projections by the Social Security Administration.

PART SEVEN

Personal Incomes

Real compensation per hour has risen roughly in line with real output per hour.

A fundamental principle of economic theory, to which most economists subscribe, is that an employer who wishes to maximize profit will hire labor up to the point where what the worker produces equals the going wage. Rooted in the theory of the firm, the principle assumes that the wages, prices, and technology are given and are not expected to change. In a world of changing prices, expectations, and technology, and rigidities of all kinds, it is far from certain that the theory holds for the entire economy on an annual basis. Yet data for manufacturing as a whole and for business have indicated a close relationship between trends in productivity and trends in real wages. Empirical investigations of growth in the United States have used this principle for their theoretical underpinning.

The two charts on page 105 show postwar trends in output per man-hour and real compensation per man-hour for the private business sector. In the top chart, real compensation per man-hour is obtained by dividing current dollar compensation per hour by the price index of the Bureau of Economic Analysis for personal consumption expenditures. It is an employee welfare measure, which tells us something about the buying power of an hour of labor of an average worker. It is not the only measure, however, that might be used, as we suggest below. The top chart illustrates clearly that the slowdown in the growth of productivity since the early 1970s has its counterpart in the behavior of real compensation. The relationship holds not for short periods, such as a year or two, but for extended periods.

The top chart also shows a widening gap between the growth of productivity and the growth of real wages. The gap is much smaller, however, when real compensation is calculated with a price index that measures the price of what the average worker has produced in an hour. This is illustrated in the bottom chart, which deflates current dollar compensation with BEA's chain-type price index applicable to all private business output.

OUTPUT PER HOUR AND REAL COMPENSATION PER HOUR IN THE BUSINESS SECTOR, 1948–1997

INDEXES: 1948=100

Compensation per Hour Adjusted by Price Index
for Personal Consumption Expenditures

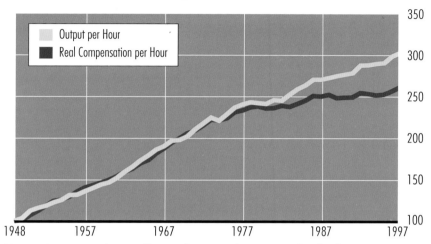

Note: Output per hour reflects adjustment by price index for business output.

Compensation per Hour Adjusted by Price Index
for Business Output, 1948–1997

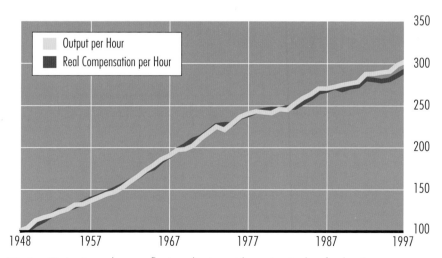

Note: Output per hour reflects adjustment by price index for business output.

Different definitions and measurements yield different pictures of recent developments in real wages.

Finding out how much real wages have changed over time becomes complicated because definitions vary and different measures may be found for any particular definition. A *real wage* is so many dollars of pay per hour or week or year divided by a price index. In this country, several choices are available for both numerator and denominator. The numerator may refer to wages only, wages and salaries only, or wages and salaries plus fringe benefits. This last, more inclusive measure is labeled *employee compensation* in the U.S. national income accounts. Because for many years workers have shown a preference for fringe benefits rather than for pay increases (see page 40), this analysis focuses on employee compensation per hour. The charts on pages 105 and 107 use compensation per hour as estimated by the BLS in its multifactor productivity database.

On the opposite page, the top chart compares the two measures of real compensation per hour that appear in the charts on page 105. From 1973 to 1997, both show a considerable slowdown as compared with the change from 1948 to 1973. The slowdown is more pronounced with the employee welfare measure. Since the numerators are the same, an explanation of the difference must be found in the price indexes, which are illustrated in the bottom chart on page 107.

Why has the price index for business output gone up less than the price index for personal consumption expenditures, and why has the difference widened in the more recent period? We do not have the complete answer, but it is partly a reflection of the increased importance of information technology—with its rapid productivity gains—in the production of capital goods in this country. From 1973 to 1998, a period of considerable price inflation, the price of information-processing equipment—computers, peripherals, communication equipment, copiers, and so forth—declined by about one-half. Because computers have less importance in total consumer spending than in business output, that price decline has had a greater dampening effect on the price rise of business output. And although inflation subsided in the 1990s, prices of information-processing equipment fell at a faster rate than before.

TWO MEASURES OF REAL COMPENSATION PER HOUR IN THE BUSINESS SECTOR, 1948–1997

INDEXES: 1948=100

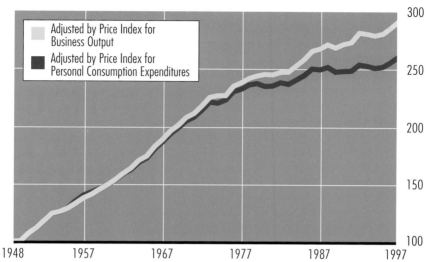

Legend:
- Adjusted by Price Index for Business Output
- Adjusted by Price Index for Personal Consumption Expenditures

(Y-axis: 100, 150, 200, 250, 300; X-axis: 1948, 1957, 1967, 1977, 1987, 1997)

PERSONAL CONSUMPTION PRICE INDEX AND PRIVATE BUSINESS OUTPUT PRICE INDEX, 1948–1997

INDEXES: 1948=100, LOGARITHMIC SCALE

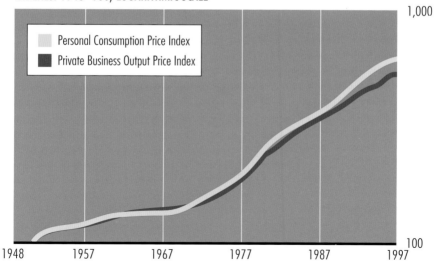

Legend:
- Personal Consumption Price Index
- Private Business Output Price Index

(Y-axis: 100, 1,000; X-axis: 1948, 1957, 1967, 1977, 1987, 1997)

Some commonly used measures give an inaccurate picture of the course of real employee compensation in recent decades.

The best-known measures of real wages are the long-established Bureau of Labor Statistics series on real average *hourly* earnings and real average *weekly* earnings of "production and nonsupervisory employees" in private nonfarm industries. In the chart, the dark line depicts the course of average hourly earnings, obtained by deflating current dollar earnings by the consumer price index. From 1973 to 1998, this series decreases at an annual rate of 0.4 percent per year, after having increased at a rate of 2.3 percent per year from 1948 to 1973. The light line—real average weekly earnings—declines even more than the hourly series.

Though useful for some purposes, those measures are not good indicators of long-run changes in the real buying power of an hour or week of work for all private industry employees. For example, the two series charted on page 109 cover wages only, which have risen less than fringe benefits. According to the comparatively new BLS index of employment costs, from December 1980 to December 1998 average wages and salaries in private industry (before adjustment for inflation) went up 4.1 percent per year, but average compensation including fringe benefits rose 4.4 percent per year. Before 1983, the CPI overstated the rise in consumer prices because of the way it measured housing costs—an old fault often ignored in making long-term comparisons. Other qualifications to the CPI are discussed in the section dealing with the quality of life. As for average weekly earnings, they have declined to some extent because many workers, new to the labor market, have chosen to work a short week. (See the discussion about part-time work on page 94.)

Those shortcomings notwithstanding, there is no denying that workers covered by the BLS series illustrated in the chart have done less well than all private employees. In the past two decades, wage or compensation increases of blue-collar workers have lagged behind those for all private industry employees. Persons in the upper part of the income distribution have fared better, as is discussed in part eight on income distribution.

CONVENTIONAL MEASURES OF REAL EARNINGS IN PRIVATE NONAGRICULTURAL INDUSTRIES, 1947–1998

INDEXES: 1982=100

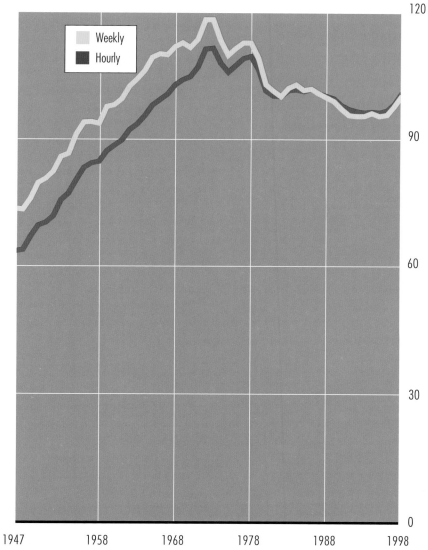

Slower productivity growth is reflected in a slower rise in family real income. Using better price measures and accounting for smaller family size improve the estimated results.

Since the growth of real labor compensation per hour or year has slowed down, the growth of any other income measure consisting mainly of labor compensation—such as the income of most families—also exhibits a slowdown. When Census Bureau data from the Current Population Survey on median family cash income are deflated by the consumer price index (CPI-U), they rise only 4 percent from 1973 to 1997, as shown in the bottom line on page 111. But these results must be qualified. The official CPI overstates the price rise; in addition, family size has decreased by 0.4 persons per family over this period.

The middle line of the chart deflates median money income by an alternative BLS price index, CPI-U-RS. This research index reflects most of the improvements made in the CPI since 1973, notably a superior method for calculating housing costs (introduced in 1983 but available for research purposes back to 1967) and an improved index number formula (introduced in 1999). When the BLS makes an improvement in calculating the CPI, it does not go back to change the published, historical "official" figures, but revised figures are clearly needed to see the effect of statistical improvements. Thus, to quote the BLS, the CPI-U-RS tries to answer the question What would have been the measured rate of inflation since 1973 if the improved methods in use in 1999 had been in use since that year?

Finally, the top line reflects the additional adjustment for smaller family size and changes in family composition. With the price index and family-size adjustments, real family income rose about 17 percent from 1973 to 1997. Median income reached a peak in 1989 and declined about 6 percent as a result of the recession and the weak recovery in 1992 and 1993. However, by 1997, it had come back to the high attained in 1989 and rose further in 1998.

Despite the new views and research regarding price change, there can be little doubt that a slowdown in the growth of family real income has occurred since the earlier postwar period. Measurement of the longer historical record needs improvement; until it is improved, it is hard to be precise about the size of the slowdown, not to mention its causes.

MEDIAN FAMILY INCOME, WITH ADJUSTMENTS, 1973–1997

INDEXES: 1973=100

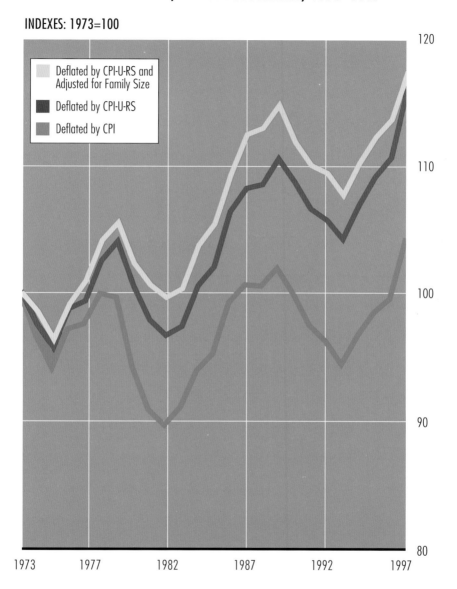

PART EIGHT

Distribution of Income

As has been true in all times and all places, the distribution of income in the United States is unequal. The change in the United States in the past twenty years is hard to interpret.

The universally observed inequality in the distribution of income reflects the unequal distribution of the factors that yield income: personal productivity, attitudes toward work and saving, inherited wealth, power, and luck. The distribution of income—after taxes and including government benefits— may also be significantly influenced by the size and character of these factors.

The chart shows the distribution of income becoming increasingly unequal among families in the standard measurement by the Census Bureau from 1976 to 1997. The share of total income received by all families except the fifth of families with the highest incomes declined. These figures do not account for taxes and noncash benefits for food and housing and are not adjusted for family size. These corrections are not available for the most recent years. For the earlier years for which they are available, they also show an increase in inequality, but a smaller one than indicated in this chart. The charts on page 119 show how the estimates of income distribution depend on how income is measured.

An important qualification to the figures shown here is that they relate to the income received by a family in a single year, whereas income received over a longer period, up to a lifetime, is certainly more equally distributed and more significant as a measure of family welfare.

The distribution of income results from differences among people in factors that affect income and differences in the income of people with the same characteristics. Inequality of family income is partly a matter of age. Even if everyone had the same income over a lifetime, annual incomes would be unequal because people in their prime working years would earn more than younger and older people. Not only is the distribution of income at a particular time influenced by the differences in the earnings of people of different ages, but the change in the distribution of income is influenced by the changes in the age distribution of the population.

The additional income earned for additional education has increased. Because the higher-income persons tend to be the better educated, that factor has increased their relative income. Change in family structure is also important. The lowest quintile has been increasingly populated by young unmarried women with low productivity, while the highest quintile is increasingly populated by families with two employed and educated adults.

SHARES OF INCOME OF HOUSEHOLDS BY QUINTILE, 1976–1997

PERCENT OF TOTAL INCOMES

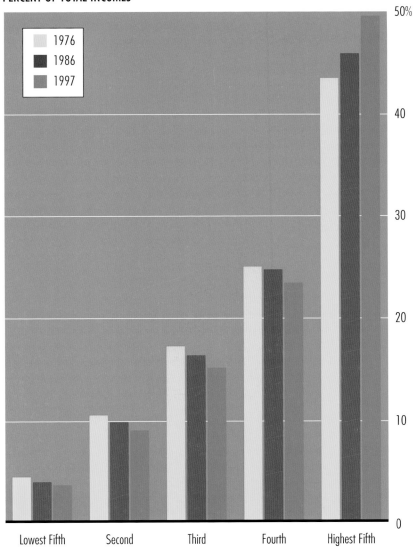

FAMILIES RANKED BY INCOME

Estimates of the distribution of income depend heavily on the definition of *income*.

The chart shows, for 1996, the proportion of all households with incomes in four income brackets under four of the definitions of income employed by the Bureau of the Census. The definitions follow:

1. Money income (excluding capital gains)
2. Definition 1 less government transfers, plus capital gains, plus health insurance supplements
3. Definition 2 less net taxes, plus net transfers
4. Definition 3 plus net imputed return on equity in own home

Under the first definition, money income, 20 percent of households had incomes less than $15,000. But if government transfers are subtracted from their incomes, the second definition, the proportion is 28 percent. If we add back transfers and account for net taxes, which are negative for low-income people because of the earned income credit, the third definition, the proportion with incomes less than $15,000, falls to 16 percent.

At the other end of the distribution, in counting money income alone before taxes, 8 percent of the households had incomes exceeding $100,000. Adding in capital gains and health insurance supplements would raise the proportion to 9 percent. But subtracting net taxes (definition 4) reduces the proportion to 5 percent.

As seen from the heights of the bars, the effect of the taxes and transfers is to reduce the proportion of households in the highest- and lowest-income categories and to raise the proportions in the two middle categories.

INCOME DISTRIBUTION BY VARIOUS DEFINITIONS OF INCOME, 1996

PERCENT OF HOUSEHOLDS

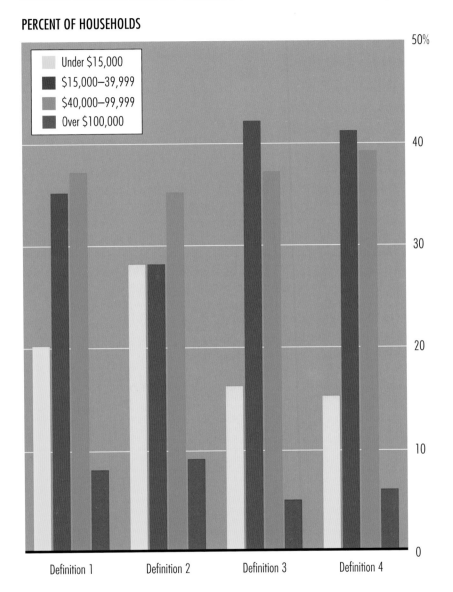

The distribution of annual consumption expenditures is less unequal than the distribution of annual income and may not be getting more unequal.

A household's annual consumption expenditures may be a better reflection of its economic condition than its income in any particular year. A household will tend to adjust its consumption expenditures to its income over a period longer than a year, as it borrows or saves less when its income is low and saves more when its income is high. Thus, its consumption expenditures represent its income over a period more significant for its welfare than for the income of a particular year. Also, surveys of households seem to get more accurate answers to questions about expenditures than to questions about incomes.

The two charts compare estimates of the distribution of expenditures and of income. It can be seen that the distribution of expenditures is much less unequal than the distribution of income. In 1995, for example, the expenditures of the richest quintile of the population were 5.2 times as large as the expenditures of the poorest quintile. The income ratio in the same year was 13.3 to 1.0. Also, the ratio for expenditures of the top to the bottom quintile barely increased, from 5.1 to 5.2. The corresponding ratio for income, however, rose from 10.4 to 13.3.

SHARES OF EXPENDITURES OF HOUSEHOLDS BY QUINTILE, 1973–1995

PERCENT OF TOTAL EXPENDITURES

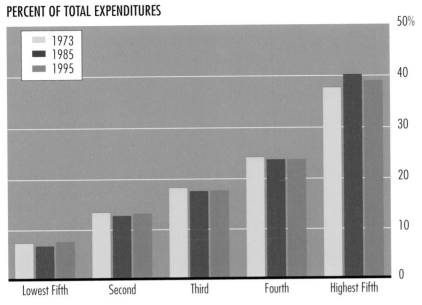

HOUSEHOLDS RANKED BY EXPENDITURES

SHARES OF INCOME OF HOUSEHOLDS BY QUINTILE, 1973–1995

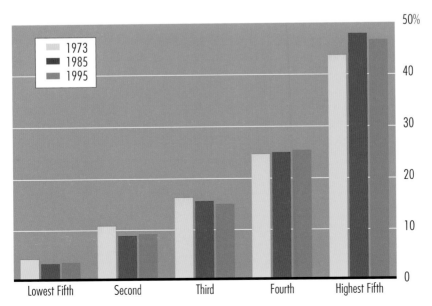

HOUSEHOLDS RANKED BY INCOME

The incomes of households with young household heads, relative to those headed by householders in their prime earning years, have declined.

Households with heads aged forty-five to fifty-four typically have higher earnings than those with either younger or older heads. That characteristic is natural, since the younger householders have less experience and education than the middle-aged ones, and many of the older ones are wholly or partially retired.

The disparity of the young relative to the middle-aged has been increasing. In 1967, households headed by persons from fifteen to twenty-four years of age had incomes equal to 62 percent of those headed by middle-aged persons. By 1997, the ratio had fallen to 43 percent. The ratios also fell, though not so much, for the twenty-five-year to thirty-four-year class and for the thirty-five-year to forty-four-year class. This widening disparity has resulted partly from the increased premium on education and experience that has been occurring for many years. But also, at least for the fifteen- to twenty-four-year-olds, the householders are younger, and more of them are female than was the case. There has been an increasing tendency for young people, especially females, to set up households of their own, apart from their families.

In the early post–World War II years, not shown here, there was also a marked decline in the incomes of older householders relative to the middle-aged. This situation may have occurred because of earlier ages at retirement. Also, in the first two decades after World War II, the gap in education and experience between those passing the age of fifty-five and those entering the forty-five-year to fifty-four-year class may have been widening. In recent years, however, the gap between the seniors and the middle-aged has stabilized and even narrowed a little bit. The more recent aged were the beneficiaries of the rapid accumulation of work experience and of retirement benefits, including Social Security, that began after World War II.

MEDIAN INCOME OF HOUSEHOLDS, BY AGE OF HOUSEHOLDER, 1967, 1982, AND 1997

INCOME OF HOUSEHOLDS HEADED BY 45- TO 54-YEAR-OLDS=100

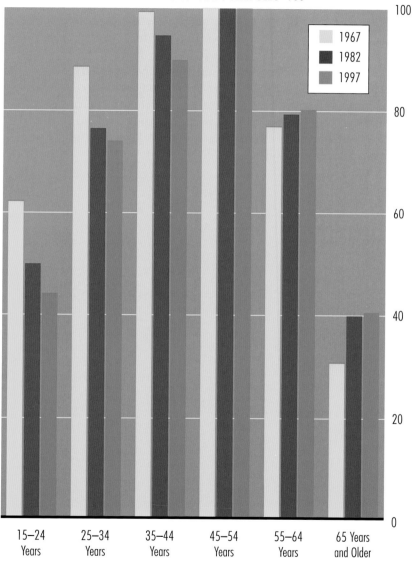

The median income of blacks and Hispanics remains significantly below the national median.

Uncertainties of definition and measurement, already noted, prevent precise statement of the absolute level and trend of median incomes. Undoubtedly, the median incomes of blacks and Hispanics are low relative to those of whites, even though the accompanying chart may not exactly measure the size of the disparity. Differences in age, family composition, education, and work experience account for some of that difference in incomes. In the case of Hispanics, the increasing number of recent immigrants may partially account for the declining relative trend. How far the differences reflect discrimination is uncertain.

MEDIAN INCOMES OF FAMILIES BY RACE, 1967–1997

PERCENT OF NATIONAL MEDIAN

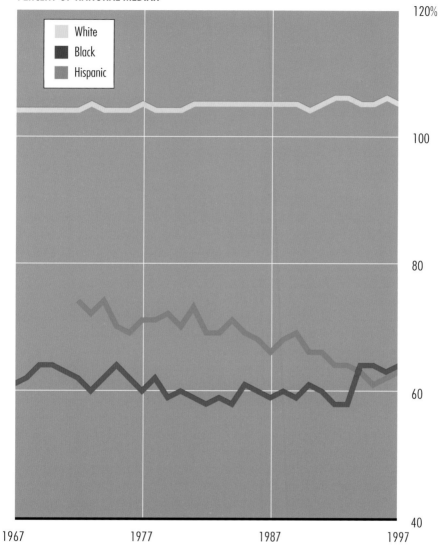

Note: Data for Hispanics not available before 1973.

The deficiency of the wages of black men compared with those of white men of similar schooling is much smaller than it was sixty years ago, but the gap has not lessened in the past twenty years.

In 1940, the average black male worker who had graduated from high school earned about 55 percent as much as a white male worker who had graduated from high school. In 1998, the black male earned about 75 percent as much. A similar reduction of the gap occurred at other levels of education. But after 1979, the disparity, though remaining much lower than in 1940, increased at the higher levels of education.

In general, the differences between the earnings of any two groups—say, blacks and whites—reflects differences in skill (productivity), differences in payment for workers of different skills (the skill differential), and differences in the payment or employment opportunities of workers with equal skills (discrimination). Although we cannot measure all these factors, clearly the big decline in the gap before 1979 was due significantly to two of them. The relative skills of black workers in each educational category increased as the schools they attended improved and as they had more work experience at jobs requiring more skill. Also, discrimination declined.

The behavior since 1979 is harder to explain. The decline of discrimination and the improvement of the relative quality of the schools attended by blacks had progressed so far that they were no longer dominant factors. At the same time, the proportion of black males who had graduated from high school or college, though still lower than that of whites, had increased much faster. The cohort of black men who had graduated, on average, might have done so more recently and had been younger and less experienced than white men. For that reason, their earnings, though rising absolutely, would have been declining relative to those of whites. That effect would have been accentuated by the economywide increase in the earnings of more skilled relative to less skilled workers. The age, experience, and skill effects may have been less important for workers who did not graduate from high school. Among them, the wages of blacks continued to rise relative to those of whites.

WEEKLY WAGES OF BLACK MALES AS A PERCENTAGE OF WHITE MALES, BY YEARS OF EDUCATION

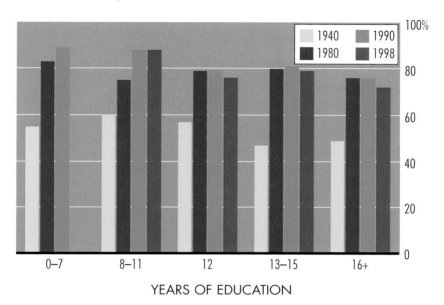

Legend: 1940, 1980, 1990, 1998

YEARS OF EDUCATION: 0–7, 8–11, 12, 13–15, 16+

WAGES OF BLACK WORKERS AS A PERCENTAGE OF WAGES OF WHITE WORKERS, BY YEARS IN THE LABOR FORCE

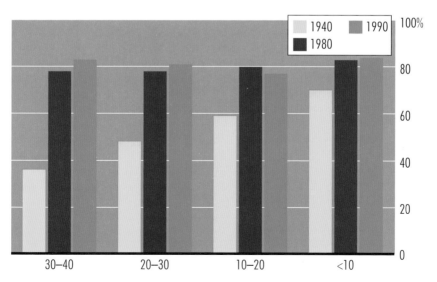

Legend: 1940, 1980, 1990

YEARS IN LABOR FORCE: 30–40, 20–30, 10–20, <10

The earnings of workers with more schooling have increased substantially, relative to the earnings of workers with less schooling.

In 1979, a male with sixteen years of schooling earned 45 percent more than one with twelve years of schooling. By 1997, the excess had risen to 73 percent. The relative increase was even greater for males with more than sixteen years of schooling—from 68 percent more than those with twelve years to 136 percent more. At the same time, the earnings of males with fewer than twelve years of schooling, relative to those with twelve years, were unchanged. Much the same picture emerges for females.

The figures cited here and shown in the charts refer to year-round full-time workers aged thirty-five to forty-four years, but the story would not be different for other age groups. Also, the figures are based on earnings excluding fringe benefits. Although we do not have comparable figures on total compensation, including fringe benefits, there is little doubt that the excess of compensation of the better educated would be as large as shown here. Probably the increase of the excess would also have been as large.

Technological change and shifts of demand toward occupations requiring more skilled workers were the main factors in this development. Increased foreign competition in markets for goods whose production requires little education may have played a part, although attempts to measure the importance of this factor have not shown it to be large. (See also page 56.)

(In the 1997 figures, workers are classified by educational attainment, such as graduation from high school or receiving a bachelor's degree. In the 1979 figures, workers are classified by years of schooling. This difference would not significantly affect the point being made here.)

MEAN INCOME OF MALES, BY YEARS OF SCHOOLING,1979 AND 1997

AS A PERCENTAGE OF MALES WITH TWELVE YEARS OF SCHOOLING

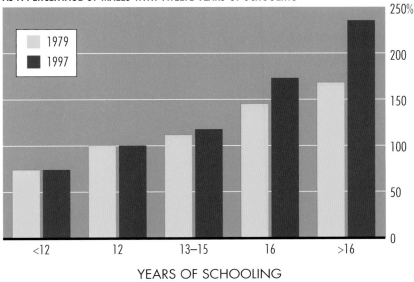

MEAN INCOME OF FEMALES, BY YEARS OF SCHOOLING, 1979 AND 1997

AS A PERCENTAGE OF FEMALES WITH TWELVE YEARS OF SCHOOLING

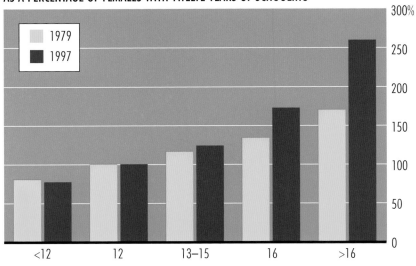

In the 1980s and 1990s, the earnings of working women have come closer to the earnings of working men.

In the twentieth century, women's earnings rose from about 45 percent of men's to more than 70 percent. This increase resulted from the rise in the educational attainment of women and from the decline of discrimination against the entry of women into some of the higher-paid occupations. Also, technological change reduced the relative earnings in jobs requiring much physical strength, which were mainly men's jobs.

This long-run trend to reduction of the "earnings gap" was interrupted in the 1960s and 1970s. The number of women in the labor force was rising much more rapidly than the number of men, so that the proportion of women with scant work experience was much larger than the proportion of men. In the past two decades, however, the factors tending to reduce the gap have again predominated, and the relative earnings of women have risen to a new high. This situation is especially true for younger women, who have entered the labor force in an environment where opportunities for advancement were most favorable.

The causes of the remaining gap are unclear. Some differences in work experience remain, as women are much more likely to have their work in the marketplace interrupted by household responsibilities. Also, women may be attracted to occupations that are congenial to them for various reasons even though their earnings may not be the highest that they could obtain. How much, if any, discrimination remains—in the sense that women are being paid less than men of similar productivity and preferences—is an unresolved question.

RATIO OF WOMEN'S TO MEN'S WEEKLY WAGES, BY LEVEL OF EDUCATION, FULL-TIME WORKERS, 1979 AND 1994

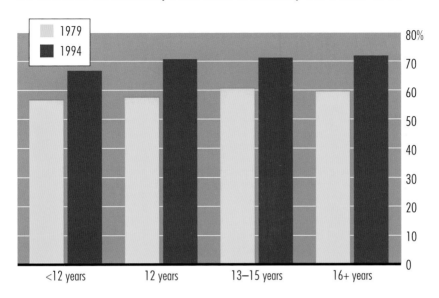

RATIO OF WOMEN'S TO MEN'S WEEKLY WAGES, BY AGE, FULL-TIME WORKERS, 1979 AND 1994

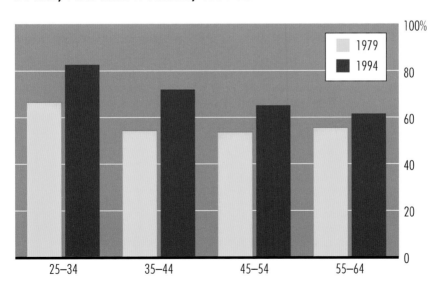

Differences in income per capita among states are large.

In 1998, per capita income in Connecticut, the state with the highest per capita income, was $37,600, or 142 percent of the U.S. average, while income in Mississippi, the state with the lowest per capita income, was $18,960, or 72 percent of the national average. Focusing on the top five and bottom five states would narrow the spread somewhat, but not much. Extremes are not the whole story. The middle part of the distribution is large: for example, thirty-two states have per capita incomes that fall within 15 percent of the national average.

The economic well-being of the average resident depends on things besides before-tax income, namely, the burden of taxation and the cost of living in different places. The only tax figures available on a basis consistent with the income data are income taxes (federal, state, and local).

The pattern of after-tax incomes does show some differences from the before-tax pattern, since state income tax rates vary among the states. By and large, though, the picture shows few differences. Federal income taxes, which are common to all states, accounted for 78 percent of combined federal, state, and local income taxes in 1998. The effective federal tax rate would, of course, be affected by differences in income distributions within states. A more accurate analysis would also take account of sales and property taxes.

Current figures on what it costs to live in different states are not available. The Bureau of Labor Statistics once published comparisons of the costs to maintain a "moderate urban living standard" for a four-person family and a two-person retired couple in each of several dozen metropolitan areas. The figures are no longer available and, in any case, were limited in scope. About all one can say is that differences in per capita incomes among states would be reduced but would still remain after taking living costs into account.

PERSONAL INCOME PER CAPITA FOR THE HIGHEST AND LOWEST STATES, 1998

THOUSANDS OF DOLLARS

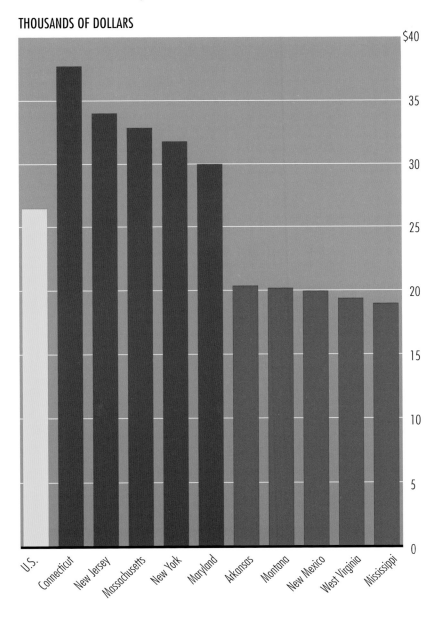

Regional disparities in income per capita have decreased.

From 1929 to 1979, differences in state per capita incomes grew smaller. In the 1940s, trends that were evident in the 1930s were greatly accelerated and continued at a slower but fairly steady pace for the next three decades. The 1980s witnessed a reversal that seems to have been short-lived, because, by the end of that decade, the long-term pattern of convergence was reasserting itself.

The chart, taken from one published earlier by the Bureau of Economic Analysis, illustrates these movements in summary form. The states were divided into eight regions. Each region was defined once as either *high income* or *low income*, depending on whether it was above or below the average income for all states. In 1929, the high group was 127 percent of the U.S. average, while the low group was 64 percent. By 1949, those differences had become 113 percent and 81 percent and, by 1979, 108 percent and 90 percent. The reversal shows up in 1989, when the high group went to 109 percent and the low to 88 percent. The resumption of the long-term trend is evident in the 1998 figures of 108 percent and 91 percent.

These numbers show how much the low-income regions—the South in particular—have improved relative to the rest of the country. Per capita incomes are still below average in the South, but that region can no longer be viewed as it was a generation ago.

High-income areas have experienced a relative decline. Many older areas in the Northeast and Midwest, where basic industries were once dominant, have stagnated. At the same time, businesses have been attracted to low-cost areas, where they have made new investments, which in turn have brought about increases in labor productivity and wages. According to conventional economic theory, regional income differences should become smaller, if not disappear completely, if resources are free to move, as they are in the United States.

INCOME PER CAPITA AS PERCENTAGE OF U.S. AVERAGE FOR HIGH– AND LOW–PERSONAL-INCOME REGIONS, 1929–1998

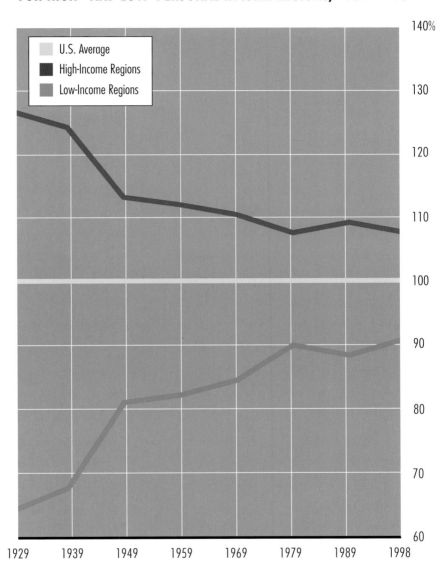

PART NINE

Poverty

There is no objective definition of *poverty* **and no objective way of measuring how many people are in poverty. The numbers differ greatly according to different plausible definitions and methods of measurement.**

The term *poverty* not only implies having less income than someone else or less income than one would like, but it means an economic condition of sufficient concern to elicit sympathy from others, and possibly to raise the question of social action to correct it. The precise nature of this condition differs in different countries, in different times, and in the judgment of different people. No single definition is possible. Even when a definition is chosen, different sources of information yield widely different answers.

Statisticians or economists cannot define poverty. They can describe only the definition being measured at the time. Others would have to decide whether that definition conforms to the picture they have in mind when they think of poverty. The chart measures the percentage of the U.S. population in poverty in a recent year by various definitions, which are far from the total range of plausible definitions. Some of these estimates are available only for years in the 1980s, but there is no reason to think that the range is significantly different today. The Census Bureau provides estimates of people in poverty by fourteen standards. Some problems of measurement are illustrated in the chart on page 139.

The definitions illustrated here follow:

A. The official standard—cash income below the official threshold of three times the cost of minimum food needs in 1963, adjusted by change in the consumer price index (1997)

B. The standard recommended by the National Research Council, based on minimum needs for food, housing, and medical care, adjusted to changing national consumption behavior (1994)

C. Similar to A but based on a sample survey of consumption, rather than on income (1989)

D. Similar to C but estimate of consumption adjusted to national income and product statistics, rather than to sample survey (1989)

E. Proportion of population reporting themselves as poor, according to opinion survey (1996)

F. Proportion of population with income below 50 percent of the median income (1984–1987)

U.S. POVERTY RATE ACCORDING TO VARIOUS DEFINITIONS OF POVERTY

PERCENT OF U.S. POPULATION BELOW POVERTY LINE

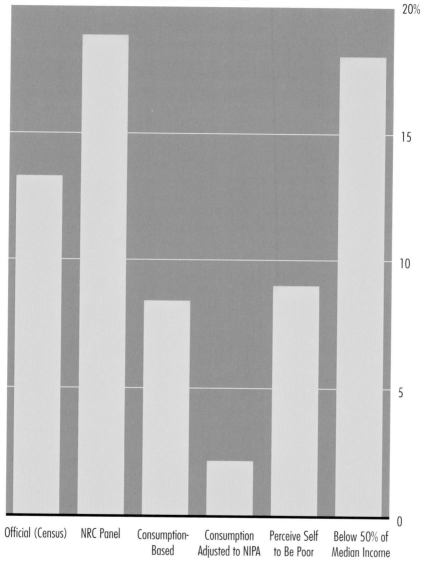

Whether poverty in America has been declining or rising in the past twenty years is uncertain, and is a matter of measurement and definition.

According to the official Census Bureau measurement of poverty, the proportion of the population in poverty fell to a low in 1978 and has fluctuated within a narrow but slightly rising range since. But according to other measurements, the rate has continued to decline. One of these alternative measurements is shown on the chart. It measures a household's resources by its reported expenditures, rather than by its reported income, partly because reports of expenditure are more likely to be accurate and partly because expenditures are less affected by short-run fluctuations. This measure also corrects the reported expenditures for what is known about total consumer expenditures from national data.

Both of these measurements are calculations of the proportion of the population whose living conditions fall below a standard of poverty first defined in the early 1960s and held constant since. Despite the uncertainties of measurement, this proportion has probably continued to fall, although the amount of the decline is uncertain.

We can, however, employ a different test. The standard of what constitutes poverty may not be regarded as a constant but as a variable that changes as conditions of life change. One could then ask whether the proportion of the population in 1998 with living conditions below the 1998 standard of poverty is lower or higher than the proportion of the 1978 population who had living conditions below the standard of 1978. But we have no unique, objective answer to that question, because we have no unique, objective way of determining how the standard changes over time.

The number of people in poverty is sometimes considered the number with incomes below some constant fraction of the median income. This outlook converts the measurement of the change in poverty to a measurement of the change in the distribution of income. The distribution question, along with the uncertainty about whether the distribution has become more unequal, was discussed in the preceding sections.

THE OFFICIAL CENSUS POVERTY RATE AND THE NIPA-CALIBRATED POVERTY RATE, 1947–1997

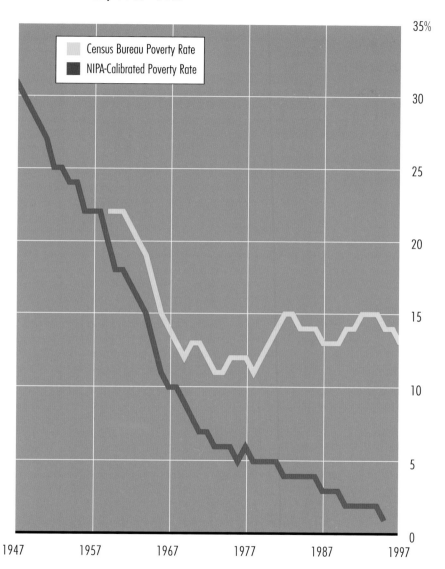

Census Bureau Poverty Rate
NIPA-Calibrated Poverty Rate

When a single absolute poverty level is used for all countries, the proportion of the population below that level is lower in the United States than in other advanced countries.

What constitutes "poverty" clearly differs from country to country and from culture to culture. Efforts have been made to calculate what proportion of the population of various countries has incomes below the level of income that would constitute poverty in the United States. For the purpose of this calculation, a "poverty line" has been estimated for the United States—it is somewhat higher than the official poverty line. Calculations for the mid-1980s showed that the proportion of the population in poverty was higher in all countries studied except Canada—and in most of the countries studied, much higher.

Another approach to international comparison of the extent of poverty is to ask what proportion of the population in each country has incomes below some fraction—say, 50 percent—of the median income in that country. When that is done, the poverty rate in the United States turns out to be higher than in most other countries studied. The explanation, of course, is that the median income in the United States is higher than in the other countries, so that a poverty level defined as 50 percent of the median is a higher income in the United States than elsewhere.

ABSOLUTE POVERTY RATES IN SELECTED COUNTRIES, MID-1980s

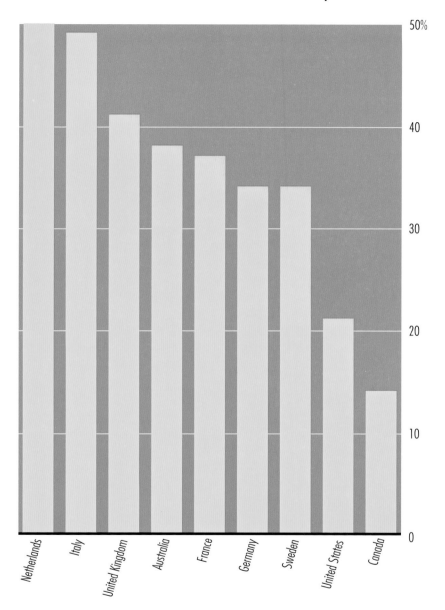

Relative to the poverty rate in the nation as a whole, the poverty rate among blacks has declined substantially since 1973 but remains high.

Because of statistical uncertainties already noted, we do not present here an estimate of the level and trend of poverty in different racial groups. The available Census Bureau measurements are, however, reasonably reliable as estimates of the *relative* poverty rate in different segments of the population. The accompanying chart shows the poverty rate of blacks, whites, and Hispanics compared with the rate in the nation as a whole.

Most striking is that the poverty rate among blacks has declined from almost three times as high in 1973 to about twice as high in 1997. This decline in the relative poverty rate of blacks is in part a consequence of the rise in the relative poverty rate of Hispanics, whose rate now exceeds that of blacks. The condition of the Hispanic population reflects, among other things, the relative youth of the Hispanic population and the increasing proportion who are recent immigrants.

What these relative figures mean for the absolute condition of blacks depends on what is true of the poverty estimates for the nation as a whole. If the official figures are correct, there has been a decline of about 20 percent in the poverty rate of blacks since 1973. But other estimates, like that on page 139, suggest that the national rate has declined since 1973 much more than is officially estimated. If these other estimates are correct, and the decline of the *relative* poverty rate of blacks shown here can be applied to them, the decline of the absolute black poverty rate was also much greater than is officially estimated.

None of these uncertainties, however, cast doubt on the observation that the poverty rate among blacks and Hispanics is much greater than it is among whites.

POVERTY RATES, BY RACE, 1959–1997

PERCENT OF NATIONAL POVERTY RATE

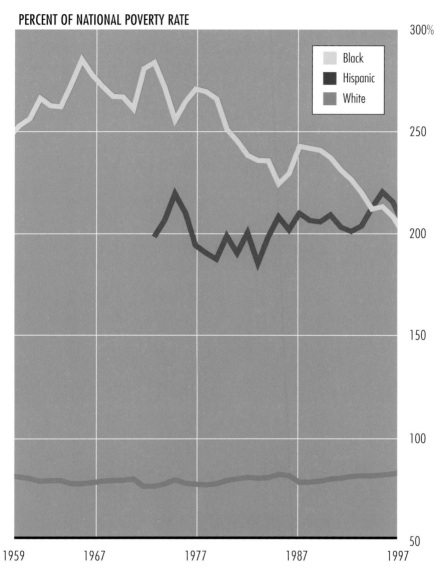

Note: Statistics for Hispanics begin in 1973.

Poverty in America has increasingly become a problem of persons in families headed by females. In 1968, 28 percent of the population in poverty were in families headed by women. By 1997, this proportion had risen to 38 percent, although the poverty rate among female-headed families, relative to the national rate, had not risen. In fact, relative to the national rate, the poverty rate in female-headed families had fallen. The proportion of the population in female-headed families had increased, however, from 9 percent to 12 percent.

The other significant change in the distribution of poverty in America was the sharp drop—from 18 percent to 9 percent—in the proportion of the poverty population who were older than sixty-five. This drop occurred despite some increase in the proportion of the elderly in the total population. The drop resulted from a decline in the poverty rate among the elderly compared with the national poverty rate. In 1968, the poverty rate among the elderly had been almost twice the national rate. By 1997, it had fallen to less than four-fifths of the national rate. Social Security undoubtedly contributed to this decline, but so did private savings and pensions.

(The foregoing statements rely on the Census Bureau estimates of the *relative* rates of poverty among classes of the population but do not imply acceptance of the bureau's estimate of the national poverty rate.)

COMPOSITION OF POVERTY POPULATION AS PERCENTAGE OF TOTAL, 1968 AND 1997

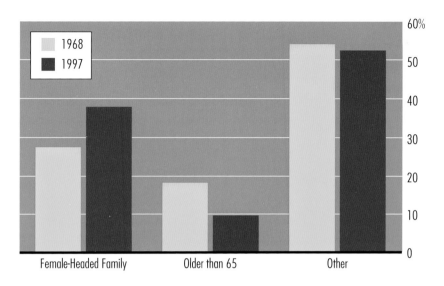

GROUP POVERTY RATES AS PERCENTAGE OF NATIONAL POVERTY RATE, 1968 AND 1997

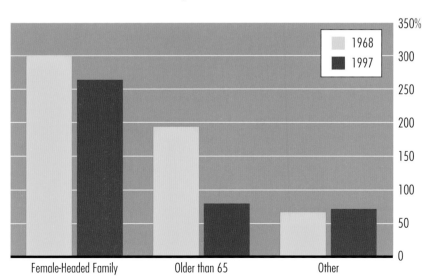

The poverty population includes a smaller group, sometimes called the *underclass*, that constitutes a special problem.

To say that a person is "in poverty" commonly suggests that he not only has a low income but also lives in a community characterized by extremely bad economic and social functioning. That is true, however, of only a small fraction of the Americans officially counted as being in poverty. That fraction is sometimes called an *underclass*, referring to permanent features, not of the persons themselves, but of the environment in which they are living.

One definition of *underclass* is people living in neighborhoods where there are significantly above-average proportions of (1) men not attached to the labor force, (2) teenagers who are high school dropouts, (3) families headed by women with children, and (4) families dependent on welfare. The chart shows the proportion of the total U.S. population and of whites and blacks separately who were in the underclass by this definition in 1970, 1980, and 1990. (Estimates for a year after 1990 will not be available until the census for the year 2000 is completed.) The numbers are much smaller than the proportion of the population officially reported as being in poverty. (The uncertainties about the official measurement of poverty have been noted on previous pages and should be recalled here.) In 1990, the numbers estimated in the underclass were less than 10 percent of the numbers reported as in poverty for the population as a whole—about 3 percent for whites and about 16 percent for blacks.

The proportion of the population living in distressed areas was higher in 1990 than in 1970. The proportion declined, however, between 1980 and 1990. That was mainly because a decline in school dropout rates removed a number of areas from the underclass category.

PERCENTAGE OF POPULATION LIVING IN "UNDERCLASS" AREAS, 1970, 1980, AND 1990

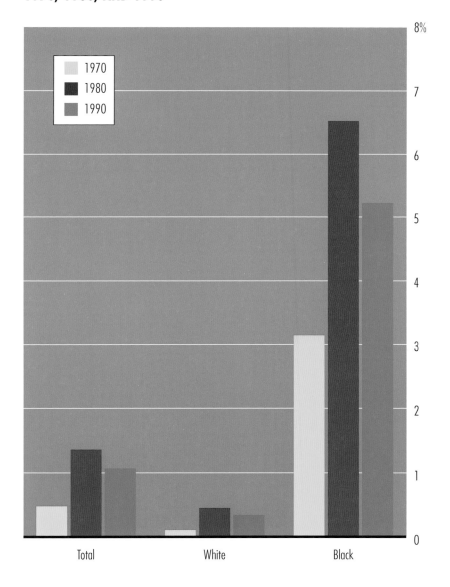

PART TEN

The Structure of the Economy

More than half of U.S. workers are employed in firms with fewer than 500 employees. In manufacturing, the importance of the largest firms varies, depending on the criterion used to measure size.

Small business occupies a prominent place in the public policy agenda of this country, a position that was formalized by the creation of the Small Business Administration in 1953. *Small business* is not an economic term: what is small in one industry may be large in another. For practical reasons, the Small Business Administration in its statistical work classifies an industry as "dominated by small business if at least 60 percent of the industry's employment is in firms with fewer than 500 employees." By that definition, U.S. business on average is not dominated by small businesses, since firms with fewer than 500 employees accounted for 52 percent of paid employment in 1995. The only industry divisions meeting the criterion of domination by small businesses were wholesale trade, retail trade, and construction. As might be expected, mining, manufacturing, transportation, and public utilities were the areas most dominated by large companies.

Measuring the size of firms, though, poses problems. For one thing, statistics for the smallest firms—those with no paid employees—are nonexistent for some industry divisions and may not be of good quality in others, because it is common for many small businesses to understate their income (judging, that is, from studies made by the Internal Revenue Service). For another, different measures of size can give different results, although that may not be a serious problem within a narrowly defined industry.

The use of employment to measure size can understate the importance of large companies, which typically have funds to make investments in fixed capital. A more significant measure of size than employment is value added or national income produced. The bottom chart illustrates the importance of the 200 biggest manufacturing firms when different size criteria are used.

PERCENTAGE OF FIRMS AND PERCENTAGE OF EMPLOYEES, BY SIZE OF FIRM, 1995

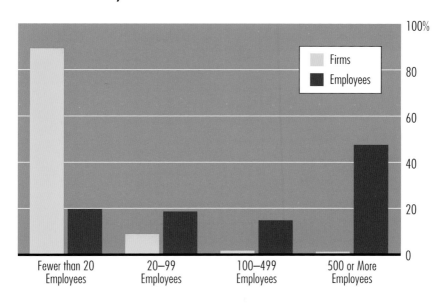

SHARES OF MANUFACTURING ACCOUNTED FOR BY 200 LARGEST FIRMS, 1992

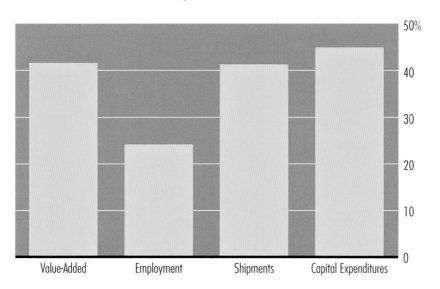

Concentration trends have been mixed. Concentration in manufacturing has changed little in recent decades, but in banking it has increased in the 1990s.

Although a few very large firms dominate several U.S. manufacturing industries, U.S. manufacturing does not appear to have become more concentrated than it was, say, in the mid-1970s. The share of value added accounted for by the 100 largest manufacturing companies rose from 23 to 33 percent between 1947 and 1963 but did not change over the next three decades (top chart).

Concentration ratios present several problems. While some firms continue to be ranked among the largest, turnover in the top group is frequent. Some firms that were household names a generation earlier are scarcely known today. High concentration ratios were supposed to signify a lack of competition, a failure of markets. On the basis of post–World War II experience, however, researchers have not been able to demonstrate a close connection between the degree of concentration and the existence of price flexibility. In addition, concentration figures have much less significance in an economy open to foreign competition than in a closed economy.

Banking, an important but much smaller part of the U.S. economy, provides an interesting contrast to manufacturing. Banking has been a highly regulated industry and has been undergoing a period of consolidation in the wake of important structural changes. The traditional commercial bank had been experiencing a significant weakening of its market position for many years, losing deposits to new types of institutions, such as money market funds, and experiencing as well a sharply decreasing share of business borrowing. In 1970, for example, commercial bank loans accounted for 38 percent of credit market debt of nonfinancial companies (excluding mortgages); by 1994, that share had fallen to 25 percent.

The most important response to these declining market shares has been an increase in merger activity, as financial institutions have sought to lower costs by expanding the scale of their operations. Since the mid-1980s, the number of commercial banks has declined by roughly one-third. After showing little change in the preceding two decades, the share of assets at the 100 largest commercial banks had risen from about one-half to two-thirds at the end of 1997 (bottom chart). And for commercial banks as a whole, the share of business borrowing started to increase significantly.

SHARES OF VALUE ADDED IN MANUFACTURING ACCOUNTED FOR BY 100 LARGEST FIRMS, 1947–1992

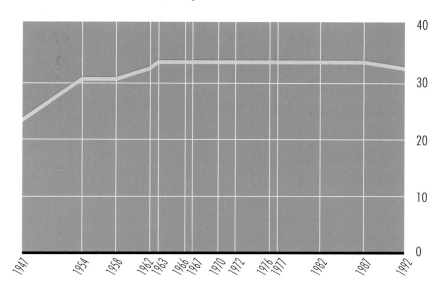

NUMBER OF U.S. COMMERCIAL BANKS AND SHARE OF ASSETS OWNED BY 100 LARGEST BANKS, 1970–1997

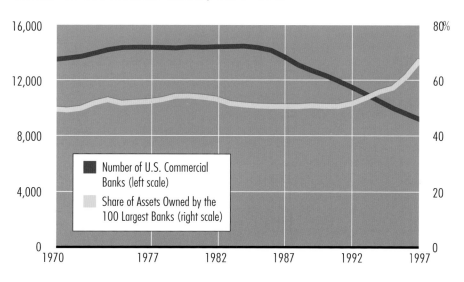

Number of U.S. Commercial Banks (left scale)

Share of Assets Owned by the 100 Largest Banks (right scale)

Several industries whose structure had been essentially fixed for much of the twentieth century are now being transformed because of a changing regulatory environment and new technology.

The communications industry provides the best-known examples. Since the breakup of the Bell System in 1984, the growth of new interstate companies employing new technology has been so rapid that, by the end of 1997, the AT&T share of operating revenues had fallen by more than one-half (top chart). The effect on prices has been striking. In June 1998, the price of interstate toll calls in the consumer price index was 26 percent lower than in May 1984, while the price of local service was 52 percent higher (bottom chart). New legislation in 1996 opened local telephone markets to competition, but the potential effect of that remains to be realized.

Over the past quarter-century or so, deregulation has extended to other industries; in the nonfinancial field, the most important are natural gas, airlines, railroads, trucking, and electric utilities. The extent of the deregulation differs from industry to industry; in varying degrees, however, regulatory authorities are no longer setting prices or controlling who may enter or exit an industry. In a setting of rising prices, deregulation has led to nominal price decreases or to real price declines, that is, price increases less than the rise in the overall price level. Resources are being used more efficiently, because prices are more closely related to costs. And, in a more competitive environment, producers have greater incentives to make use of new technologies, new marketing techniques, and other means of cutting costs, while maintaining or improving quality.

The most recent change has occurred in electric utilities, where deregulation is following a pattern used in natural gas (and other utilities). New legislation has permitted the *unbundling* of services that had typically been combined: the production or generation of electric power; its long-distance transmission; and its local distribution to the household or business. Consumers of electric power are no longer bound to purchase their power from the local utility. They will increasingly have the option of contracting with outside companies that may offer cheaper service. The new structure is expected to eliminate old high-cost producers in favor of low-cost producers employing new technologies.

AT&T SHARE OF OPERATING REVENUES OF LONG-DISTANCE CARRIERS, 1984–1997

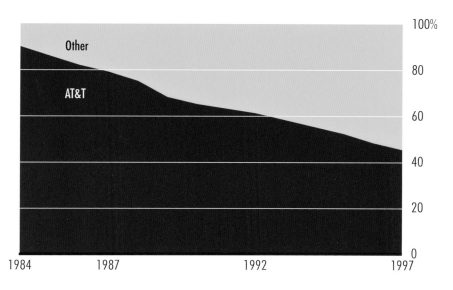

CONSUMER PRICE INDEXES FOR LOCAL AND INTERSTATE PHONE SERVICES, 1978–1998

INDEX: 1982–1984=100

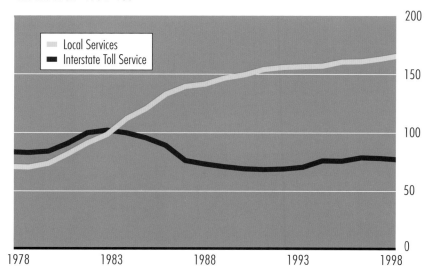

Outside of agriculture, the number of self-employed persons has been rising since the late 1960s.

Except for the early depression years, the number of self-employed persons in farming—in addition to hired farm workers—has declined almost continuously since the early part of the twentieth century, as farmers found better-paying opportunities in nonfarm work. The 1990s have witnessed a leveling off at about 1.1 million persons in farming. The 1997 figure was about one-fourth the number so classified in 1953.

Self-employed persons in nonfarm activities present a different picture. Their numbers also rose during the depression, because jobs were scarce. They rose again after World War II, because demand was strong and many veterans took advantage of the GI Bill to obtain government loans to start new businesses. Most of these businesses, however, had short lives, and the number of self-employed fell gradually until some time in the 1960s. Since that time, the number of self-employed has increased markedly, but reasons for this movement—aside from rising incomes—are not clear.

SELF-EMPLOYED PERSONS IN FARM AND NONFARM SECTORS, 1947–1997

MILLIONS OF PERSONS

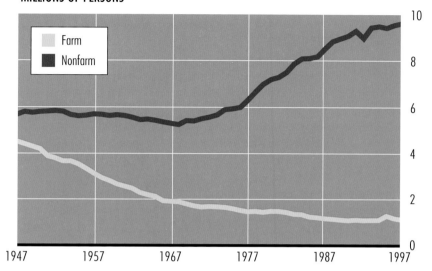

- Farm
- Nonfarm

SELF-EMPLOYED PERSONS AS PERCENTAGE OF TOTAL EMPLOYMENT IN NONFARM SECTORS, 1947–1997

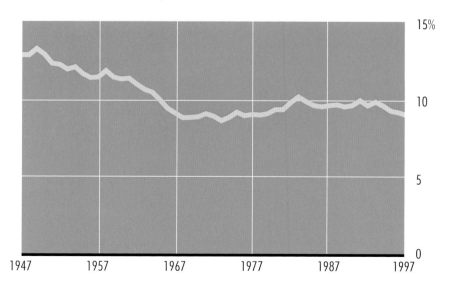

Large firms as well as small firms create new jobs. The basic question is, Which jobs have the longer life?

It has been said that small business creates most new jobs. Small firms indeed are constantly creating new jobs, mainly because hundreds of thousands of new businesses, most of them tiny, are started each year. This kind of addition to employment is often referred to as *gross* job creation. The important question is, How permanent are these jobs? Experience shows that newly established firms have a brief life span, so that, on balance, the net contribution to employment, viewed over a long period, tends to be small. Large firms also create many new jobs, and since large firms tend to be well established, their new jobs tend to have greater permanence.

One way of looking at this is to examine census statistics on the share of employment accounted for by large and small firms over long periods. For manufacturing, this is illustrated in the chart. Small firms are represented by *single-unit* companies: those having only one place of business. In this example, large firms are equated with *multiunit* companies: those with more than a single place of business. Many of these multiunit firms are small, but the distinction is a useful one.

From 1929 to 1977, the share of manufacturing employment accounted for by single-unit companies declined, from 54.0 percent in 1929 to 23.6 percent in 1977. But since then, it has risen somewhat. From 1947 to 1977, the declining share reflected absolute decreases in small-firm employment and employment increases for large firms. However, from 1977 to 1992, the last year for which census data are available, employment in small firms increased, while employment in multiunit firms decreased. It is hard to say whether this reversal in small-firm share is temporary or whether it reflects a fundamental change in markets, possibly related to computer technology, which is favorable to small-scale organization. Downsizing by the largest firms was one of the features of the 1980s that continued in the 1990s, apparently at a slower pace.

Since the mid-1950s, the small-firm share in retail trade has fallen rapidly, as chains have won increasing shares of the retail market and very small retailers have found it difficult to compete.

SHARES OF MANUFACTURING EMPLOYMENT, MULTIUNIT FIRMS COMPARED WITH SINGLE-UNIT FIRMS, 1929–1992

PERCENT OF TOTAL EMPLOYEES

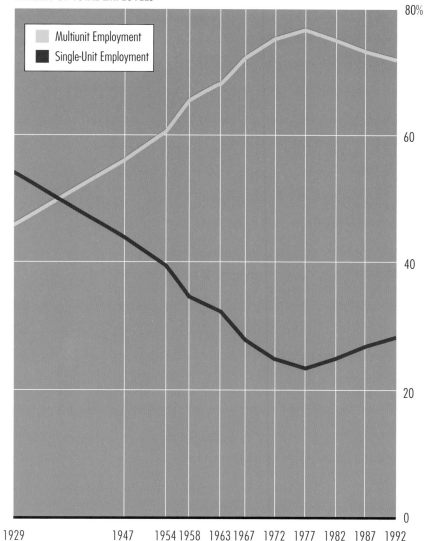

Most large U.S. industrial firms are multinational firms, with substantial operations in foreign countries.

Although this country did not invent the multinational corporation, setting up operations in foreign countries through direct investment has characterized large American companies as far back as records go. Especially early on, foreign investment came about not because this country had large amounts of capital to invest abroad, but because U.S companies had what has been called *firm-specific assets*: production know-how, patents, and brand names that came from skills in marketing and advertising.

Multinational corporations can be looked at in many ways. First, how important are parent companies in U.S. business? According to studies of the Bureau of Economic Analysis, parents of U.S. multinationals in 1997 had a GDP of more than $1.5 trillion, which represented 26 percent of U.S. private GDP, excluding banks. In manufacturing, excluding petroleum, the parent company share was 60 percent. Parent shares of total production measured in current dollars were about the same in 1997 as in 1989. However, when employment is used as the criterion, the parent share was 19 percent in 1997, compared with 20 percent in 1989. For this eight-year period, these data, after allowing for price changes, imply a rise in GDP per person employed that was well above average for the private sector. A major influence in this implied productivity increase has been the strong rise in the parent share of total private capital expenditures.

The output of $1.6 trillion associated with parent companies in 1997 exceeds $2 trillion with GDP of majority-owned foreign affiliates added in. The foreign-affiliate share of 25 percent was slightly higher than the 23 percent of 1989, but about the same as 1977. To judge from employment data, however, the 1977 share was much higher than the 1957 portion. Taken as a whole, U.S. business apparently peaked in its internationalization by 1980. Strong growth in other industrialized countries and outward investment by large native firms in countries such as Japan, Germany, and Sweden are the main reasons for the leveling in the U.S. share.

Majority-owned foreign affiliates are not large in relation to host countries. For only nine countries was the 1997 share of GDP 5 percent or more, led by Ireland at 17 percent and Canada and Singapore at 9 percent. From 1989 to 1997, the output (GDP) of affiliates grew faster than the output of low-wage host countries, but the 1997 aggregate share of GDP for such foreign affiliates in low-wage countries was still small—less than 2 percent overall.

SHARES OF MULTINATIONAL CORPORATION GROSS PRODUCT, 1977–1997

U.S. PARENTS AND MAJORITY-OWNED FOREIGN AFFILIATES

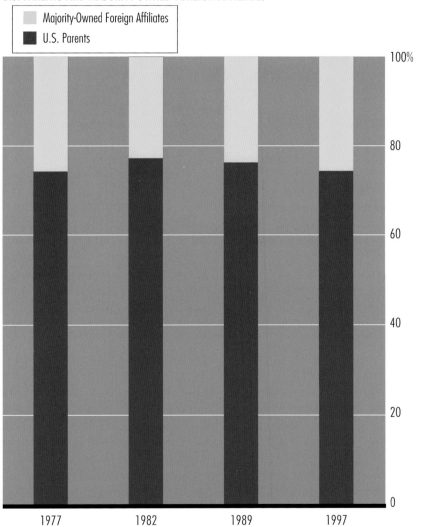

Legend:
- Majority-Owned Foreign Affiliates
- U.S. Parents

Union membership as a share of employment has declined since the 1950s.

Union membership grew in absolute numbers until about 1980, but has decreased in most years since. The period of most rapid growth was the late 1930s as a result of legislation that gave workers the right to organize. That period saw the emergence and strong rise of industrial unions.

The picture of union membership looks different when it is expressed as a share of either employment or the labor force. Unionism as a share has declined fairly steadily since the early post-World War II period. Several factors have contributed to this trend. Unions have always had their greatest impact among blue-collar employees, but factory and related workers have become relatively less important as management has substituted capital for labor. The growth of foreign investment by U.S. corporations and competition from abroad have made U.S. management less willing to recognize unions when that meant higher labor costs.

New research in the 1990s into the causes of the decline in union membership has focused on worker demand for union representation, that is, the desire, or the lack of desire, of nonunion workers for such representation. According to this research, all decline in the union share of the labor force from 1977 to 1991 could be explained by this factor alone. For this particular fourteen-year period at least, *structural change*—such as the kinds of jobs available—was found to be unimportant.

Several developments have diminished the attractiveness of union membership. New legislation and strong gains in wages and fringe benefits have doubtless contributed to job satisfaction among nonunion workers. The Employment Retirement Income Security Act of 1974 (ERISA) gave many workers the pension rights that had been won through collective bargaining. Data on employment costs from the Bureau of Labor Statistics show that, from 1979 to 1998, increases for nonunion workers have been as large as or larger than for unionized workers, whether measured by compensation as a whole, by wages and salaries alone, or by fringe benefits alone.

UNION MEMBERSHIP AS PERCENTAGE OF NONFARM EMPLOYMENT, 1930–1998

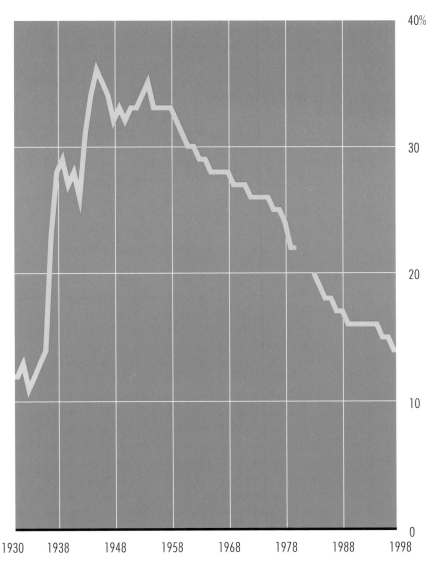

Note: Data not available for 1981–1982. Data since 1982 not strictly comparable with earlier data.

PART ELEVEN

Wealth and Debt

Many people view the behavior of the stock market as the most important indicator of the nation's economic health.

The stock market is viewed as important because a significant part of the population has some stake in the market and the behavior of no other economic indicator is so widely publicized.

More basically, the stock market as measured by price indexes such as Dow Jones Industrials (see chart) and Standard & Poor's Index of 500 stocks tends to fluctuate with business activity. Movements in those indexes reflect the changing income prospects—as viewed by the investing public—for leading American corporations, whose fortunes dominate economic activity in this country.

Market behavior can be viewed from both a short-run and long-run point of view, although it is the short run that gets most of the public's attention. Researchers who have studied business cycles give the behavior of stock prices comparatively high marks for tracking the economy. Important events in the American experience support that view, to some degree. The great stock market crash of October 1929 was a forerunner of the Great Depression of the 1930s; some economists believe that the crash itself was responsible for the depth and duration of the downturn. Although, historically, most extended declines in the stock market have foreshadowed declines in the economy, not all declines in stock prices have been followed by declines in economic activity. Another shortcoming of the market as a predictor of economic activity is the lack of uniformity in the lead provided by the market. Whether the stock market declines a few months before the economy declines or a few years, makes a difference.

Despite the volatility of stock prices in the short run, in the long run the return to stocks in the United States has been substantial. Viewed as a risky investment, stock returns have been much higher than returns to bonds. In the late 1990s, this historical experience had become part of the public discussion about fundamental changes in the Social Security system, which would permit the investment of Social Security reserves in stocks rather than exclusively in Treasury bonds.

DOW JONES INDUSTRIAL AVERAGES, 1913–1998

LOGARITHMIC SCALE

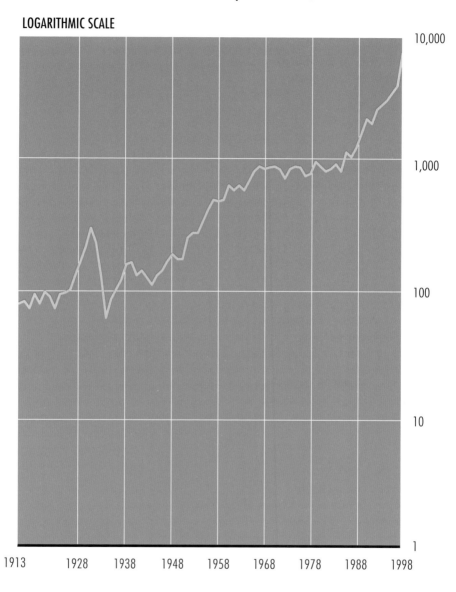

Household net worth has increased faster than GDP or disposable income since World War II, especially in the 1990s.

Net worth is the excess of assets over liabilities. According to Federal Reserve data, the net worth of U.S. households at the end of 1998 was $37 trillion. Since 1948, net worth has risen at an annual rate of 7.6 percent, as compared with a rise of 7.2 percent in either GDP or disposable personal income (top chart). Although the percentage growth in assets has been smaller than the percentage rise in liabilities over this period, net worth has grown, because, in the initial year, assets greatly exceeded liabilities. The assets underlying this calculation are the tangible and financial assets owned by households. Tangible assets embrace the estimated market value of homes, including land and other real estate, as well as the estimated replacement cost of automobiles and other consumer durables. Financial assets embrace the market value of corporate stocks that households own directly or in which they have a stake—as in employer pension funds—plus all other types of securities, cash, and owners' equity in their unincorporated businesses. The main liabilities of households are home mortgages and consumer credit.

Americans are the chief owners of American corporate business, whose stock had a market value of almost $14 trillion at the end of 1998. Holdings by foreigners were 8 percent. From 1988 to 1998, the value of corporate stocks owned by households in one form or other quintupled; this increase was far greater than in other types of assets. Corporate stocks underlying total household assets were 13 percent of those assets in 1988 and 32 percent in 1998.

The rapid growth in the value of corporate stock is why household net worth grew so much faster than GDP from 1988 to 1998: 7.2 percent per year, compared with 5.4 percent for GDP. The differential growth, in turn, was mainly a reflection of the much faster rise in stock prices than in the price of GDP, as shown in the bottom chart, which compares over ten-year intervals annual rates of change in the chained price index for GDP with those of the Standard & Poor's price index of 500 stocks. The difference in growth rates between the two indexes would give a real change in the S&P. We make no attempt to explain why stock prices have risen so rapidly in the 1990s, a situation that has baffled most, if not all, economists and stock market analysts for many years.

HOUSEHOLD NET WORTH AND GDP, 1945–1998

BILLIONS OF DOLLARS, LOGARITHMIC SCALE

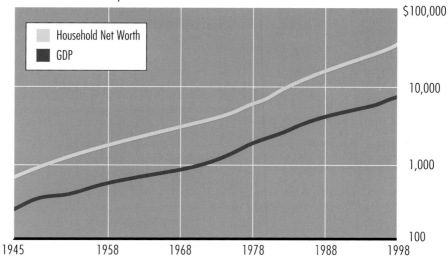

ANNUALIZED GROWTH RATE OF THE GDP CHAINED PRICE INDEX AND S&P 500 COMPOSITE INDEX, 1948–1998

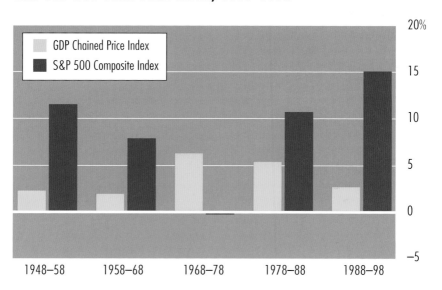

Forty-one percent of families owned stocks directly or indirectly in 1995, with a median value of $13,500, according to the most recent Federal Reserve survey. Since then, these figures have risen.

Fifteen percent of American families and individuals owned publicly traded stocks directly, according to the 1995 Federal Reserve Survey of Consumer Finances, the latest available. Since the early postwar period, the proportion of the population owning stocks directly has been growing but not steadily, according to surveys by the New York Stock Exchange. After the oil shock of 1973, stock prices fell; with only a partial recovery in prices during the 1970s, the stock-owning proportion declined. With the recovery of the stock market in the early 1980s, the proportion resumed a rise that gained momentum in the 1990s.

Besides holding stocks directly, families and individuals may hold stocks in other forms: in mutual funds whose assets are stocks (equity funds); in retirement accounts, such as Keogh accounts, individual retirement accounts (IRAs), and employer-sponsored retirement savings accounts such as 401(k) accounts; and in personal trusts and other managed-investment accounts. When stock-holding includes these other forms, the percentage holding stocks in 1995 expands to 41 percent. That proportion is substantially higher than the 32 percent share in 1989. In view of the robust stock market from 1995 to 1998, the share probably grew significantly after 1995. For example, the number of individual mutual fund accounts invested in corporate equities rose by 46 percent from 1995 to 1997, according to the Investment Company Institute.

Families that own stocks as described above tend to have higher incomes, more wealth, and more education than the population at large. According to the 1995 Federal Reserve survey, five out of six families with incomes of $100,000 or more were stock owners. As the chart on page 171 indicates, proportions were also large for families in the income classes between $25,000 and $100,000. However, the median size of holdings is small until the $50,000 income class is reached.

Changes from 1989 to 1995 in the proportion of families owning stocks in any form have occurred in all income classes, but have been especially large for families with below-average incomes. For example, for families with incomes between $10,000 and $25,000, the share approximately doubled, from 13 percent to 25 percent.

PERCENTAGE OF FAMILIES WITH DIRECT OR INDIRECT STOCK HOLDINGS AND MEDIAN VALUE OF HOLDINGS, BY FAMILY INCOME, 1995

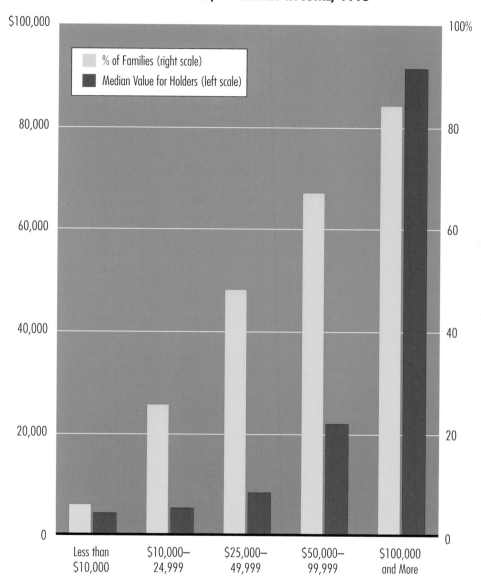

Ownership of corporate stock broadened with the growth of employer pension plans and mutual funds.

The nature of stock ownership underwent a profound change in the post–World War II period. In the early postwar years, stock ownership by individuals and personal trusts meant ownership by middle-class and wealthy people. That pattern was changed by the growth of private and state and local government pension funds, whose beneficiaries are workers of all types, blue-collar as well as white-collar.

In 1948, stock and equity mutual fund shares held directly by households accounted for 92 percent of the value of all corporate equity holdings in the United States; mutual fund shares—owned principally by households—were quite small. So were stocks in the reserves of all pension funds of private employers and state and local governments; these were only 3 percent of the total.

Over the next half-century, all types of holdings expanded, but at different rates. As a result of the rapid growth of the mutual fund industry, stock held by mutual funds constituted more than 16 percent of total corporate equities in 1998 (see chart). Pension funds expanded as employees took pay increases in the form of pension benefits (see page 40); the growth of private employer plans was especially strong from the late 1960s to the mid-1980s. State and local government retirement funds were often prevented by law from investing in stocks, but these limitations were gradually loosened. At the end of 1998, stocks held by private and public pension funds constituted one-fourth of the corporate equity total, or 27 percent when equity mutual funds are included. Direct holdings of stock by households dropped to 41 percent, or 52 percent including equity mutual funds.

The growth of private pension plans slowed and the share of total equities leveled off after the mid-1980s, partly because of a new emphasis on health benefits and partly because the dominant type of pension plan, the *defined benefit* (as discussed on page 100), was proving more costly than anticipated to employers. There was a new emphasis on *defined-contribution* plans. At the end of 1998, total assets of defined-contribution plans approximated those of defined-benefit plans. Employees have benefited to the extent that the value of stocks has increased in importance in these plans. By the same token, employees have taken on the risks of declines in the stock market.

PENSION FUND AND MUTUAL FUND HOLDINGS OF CORPORATE EQUITIES AS A PERCENTAGE OF ALL CORPORATE EQUITIES, 1945–1998

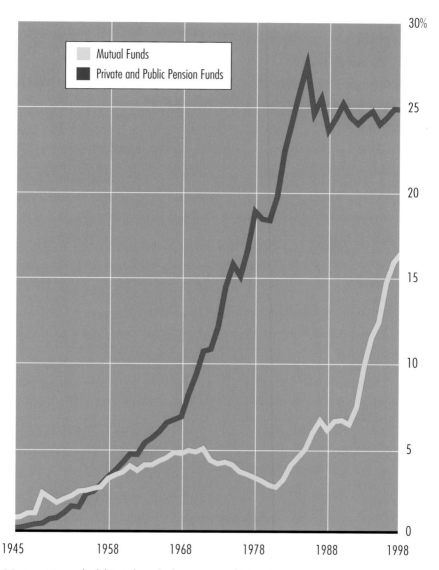

Note: Household total includes nonprofit institutions.

For much of the postwar period, the debt of nonfinancial corporations, relative to what these companies produce, has been rising.

Debt becomes burdensome during recessions, especially when downturns are deep and long-lasting. During the 1982 recession, some analysts feared either that the economy might not recover or that the recovery might be very slow because of the burden of the debt and the lack of liquidity. Such fears proved unfounded. Similar concerns about excessive credit card use and inadequate liquidity were expressed in the 1990–1991 recession, particularly in 1991 and 1992, when the recovery of the economy remained slow in the face of a considerable easing of monetary policy. Determining when debt is "excessive" is a difficult task that economists and financial analysts often face. The charts illustrate two aspects of this problem for corporate business.

The first chart shows the ratio of credit market debt to GDP for nonfinancial corporations. Although this picture does not demonstrate that nonfinancial corporations as a whole took on an amount of debt that was excessive relative to corporate output, the ratios of 1989 and 1990 were somewhat high in relation to the postwar trend. These aggregates say nothing about particular industries or parts of the country. The real estate industry, especially commercial real estate, and the New England region went through well-publicized difficulties in the early 1990s. A few years earlier, the problems were concentrated in the oil-producing regions of the country. For the nation, the debt-GDP ratio rose through the 1990s and, at the end of 1998, was slightly below the 1989–1990 average.

Liquidity problems can become acute even for companies with substantial real assets if they have cash flow troubles. The second chart shows annual net interest payments relative to cash flow, where cash flow— undistributed profits plus depreciation—is calculated on the NIPA basis. The ratios in 1989 and 1990 were much higher than in the recession years of 1974 and 1982, but they fell sharply during the 1990s and, in 1998, were lower than for any other year since 1967.

CREDIT MARKET DEBT AS PERCENTAGE OF GDP FOR NONFINANCIAL CORPORATIONS, 1945–1998

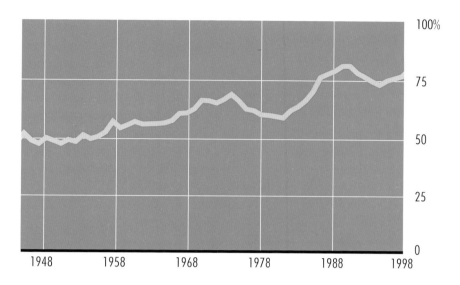

NET INTEREST AS PERCENTAGE OF CASH FLOW FOR NONFINANCIAL CORPORATIONS, 1945–1998

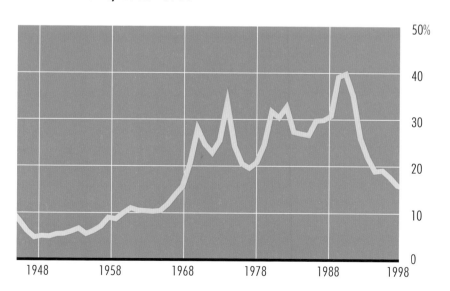

In the 1970s and 1980s, corporations increased their use of debt relative to equity for their external financing. A decline in the debt proportion did not come until the 1990s.

In the postwar period, corporations have relied much more on debt than on equity for their external financing. Tax laws have encouraged debt financing because interest costs, unlike dividends, are a deductible expense, although reductions in the corporate tax rate in the 1980s should have lessened this influence.

One factor favoring debt financing is the rate of inflation. When the rate of inflation increased in the early 1970s, the incentive of corporations to invest in plants, equipment, and inventories was strengthened, because business could borrow funds (from the household sector) at real rates of interest that were low and at times negative. In the 1960s, debt was only 28 percent of debt-plus-equity of nonfinancial corporations; in the 1970s, however, that percentage rose to 42.

Although high real interest rates and disinflation after the early 1980s should have brought about a large drop in the debt ratio, the decline was not pronounced; a significant drop did not occur until the 1990s. Economists are not entirely clear about why debt financing was favored so much in the 1980s. The use of debt may have been encouraged by the emergence of various kinds of protective devices (hedging) in financial markets generally. More-liberal bankruptcy laws in this country after 1979, as well as the spread of leveraged buyouts with junk bonds, may have affected this ratio.

RATIO OF DEBT TO THE SUM OF DEBT AND EQUITY OUTSTANDING, NONFINANCIAL CORPORATIONS, 1945–1998

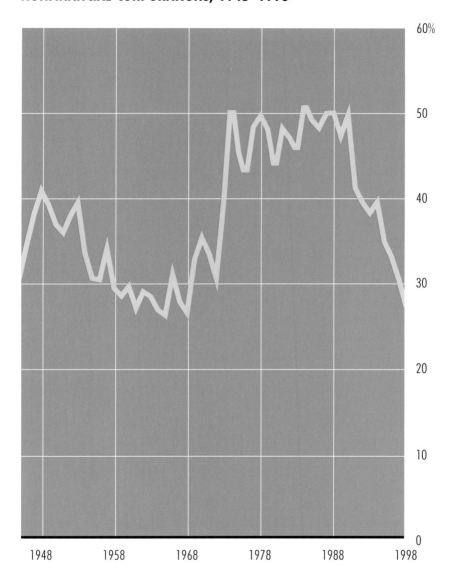

In 1995, half of U.S. households had a net worth of $56,400 or more. The ownership of wealth is highly concentrated.

The median net worth of households in 1995 was $56,400 according to the Federal Reserve. Some 30 percent of that figure represented equity in a home (the value of a home less debt). About 19 percent represented the interest in a busines or profession, while the rest was spread over various assets such as other real estate, automobiles, checking and savings accounts, individual retirement accounts, and other financial assets.

Wealth in the United States, as in most countries, tends to be concentrated. The chart, for 1995, is based on a Federal Reserve survey that pays special attention to families in the higher-income brackets. According to this survey, 26 percent of U.S. families had (1994) incomes of $50,000 or more and accounted for 69 percent of family net worth in that year. Six percent of all families—those with 1994 incomes of $100,000 or more— had 44 percent of the wealth in 1995. The share for that income group declined from 1989.

If households were ranked according to their wealth instead of their incomes, the concentration would be more pronounced. Economists have estimated that the richest 1 percent of wealth holders held at least one-fourth of the total wealth in this country in 1922–1983. Over that sixty-year span, the share held by the top 1 percent declined.

Estimates of wealth distributions have a long history and at one time were based on estate tax returns filed by wealthier individuals. The traditional focus on wealthy persons' holdings of stocks, bonds, real estate, and similar assets overlooks certain components of wealth owned by average families, such as pension wealth and automobiles. As noted on page 61, durable goods owned by households were 11 percent of all private and public capital in the United States in 1997.

Social Security wealth, which is excluded from the foregoing statistics, is an important part of wealth that should be taken into account when measuring the level and trend of wealth and its concentration. Including the capitalized value of Social Security benefits would reduce the apparent concentration of wealth and accentuate its long-term decline. This is true also of wealth represented by employer-financed private pensions. Inclusion of household durables and automobiles would likewise reduce the concentration of wealth.

1995 DISTRIBUTION OF FAMILIES AND NET WORTH BY INCOME LEVEL

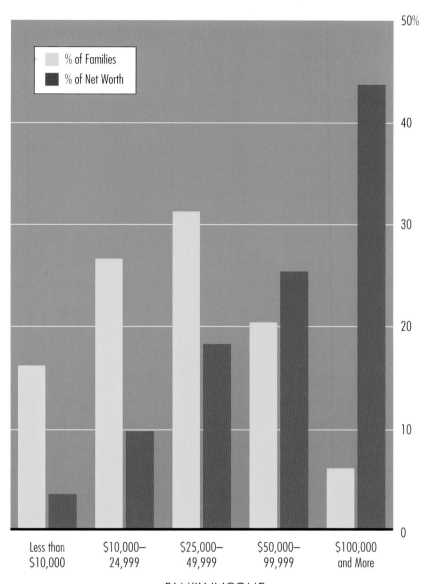

PART TWELVE

Economic Fluctuations

The U.S. economy, like most other industrial economies, fluctuates around a rising long-term growth trend. This country has experienced thirty cycles of expansion and contraction since 1854 and nine since World War II.

Fluctuations in economic activity, generally referred to as *business cycles*, have been documented in this country back to the midnineteenth century. Concern over fluctuations—contractions because they bring unemployment and expansions because they lead to inflation—has been the dominant theme of national economic policy in much of the twentieth century.

The chart plots quarterly, seasonally adjusted data for an index of coincident indicators (employment, industrial production, real personal income, and real business sales).

Economists have distinguished different phases of fluctuations. *Expansions* are marked by rising production, sales, employment, and many other aspects of economic activity, but these tend to slow down and reach a *peak*. The peak is followed by *contractions* in production and employment and by rising unemployment, until a bottom or *trough* is reached. The process repeats, in an irregular way, as the economy goes through a recovery phase and resumes another expansion, which continues until another peak is reached.

Lines of demarcation between these phases of the business cycle are often fuzzy, because the statistics contain errors and are frequently contradictory. Months may go by before it is generally recognized that a recession—or a recovery—is underway.

Theories about the causes of economic fluctuations abound. Some are related to the waves of optimism and pessimism that accompany the increases and decreases in economic activity. When sales are increasing, business spirits become buoyant and at times give rise to beliefs that the expansion will continue indefinitely. Investments that look profitable when started turn out to be unprofitable when markets weaken. Although, in the latter part of the twentieth century, economists paid increasing attention to the role of the Federal Reserve in its attempts to stabilize the economy—as discussed further on—there is no single explanation of the business cycle; it can still be said that the factors that may be important in one period are not necessarily important in another. That variation is consistent with the modern view that business fluctuations are caused primarily by random shocks to the economy—for example, the oil crisis of late 1973.

QUARTERLY BUSINESS ACTIVITY, 1948–1998

INDEX: 1992 AVERAGE=100

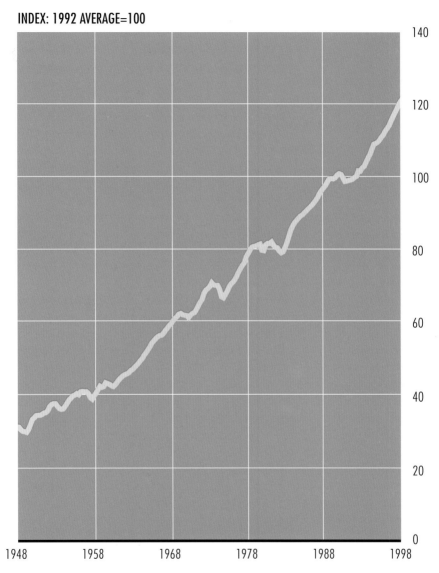

Note: Composite index of four coincident indicators

The length of fluctuations in the economy is highly uneven, and there does not seem to be any "normal" duration. But expansions are much longer than contractions.

Expansions in the postwar period have been as short as 12 months and as long as 106 months. Completed expansions have averaged 50 months, and the last full one—from November 1982 to July 1990—was very long by postwar standards. The expansion that started in April 1991 was still in progress in the summer of 1999 and had lasted longer than the preceding expansion.

Contractions fall in a much narrower range: 6–16 months, with an average of 11 months. The most recent contraction—from July 1990 to March 1991—was slightly shorter than average, but was perceived differently because the upturn in its early stages was slower than average. The fact that expansions last four times as long as contractions is an aspect of long-term growth in the economy.

Fluctuations differ not only in duration but also in degree of change. The median decline in real GDP in the postwar period has been about 2.5 percent. The largest postwar decline was the 3.7 percent decrease over the five quarters ending in the first quarter of 1975, but the most severe in intensity was the two-quarter decrease ending in the third quarter of 1980. The irregularity in expansions and contractions introduces much uncertainty in business operations and is perhaps the main reason that governments and central banks have not been notably successful in eliminating the business cycle. It is also an important reason for the rise of a large forecasting industry. Because expansions last several years, the typical forecaster, who tries to look ahead for one or two years and tends to attach considerable weight to recent trends, is more often right than wrong. But the record of economists in foreseeing turning points—dating the times when the economy will reach a peak or a trough—is not good.

LENGTH OF POSTWAR EXPANSIONS, 1945–1990

NUMBER OF MONTHS

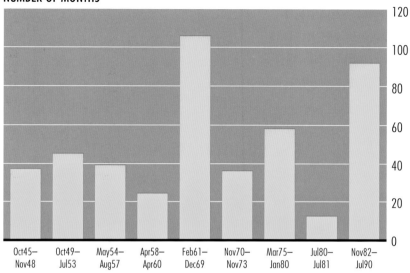

LENGTH OF POSTWAR CONTRACTIONS, 1948–1991

NUMBER OF MONTHS

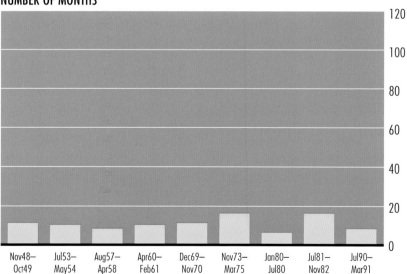

The 1929–1933 contraction was unique, as measured by the decline in output and employment and by the rise in unemployment.

The contraction of 1929–1933 lasted forty-three months, four times the length of the average post–World War II contraction. Real GDP in 1933 was some 27 percent below its 1929 level, in contrast with a median decline of 2.5 percent for the post–World War II contractions. Unemployment reached 25 percent in 1933.

Another common way of gauging recessions is to measure how much time elapses before the economy attains the output level at its previous peak. For contractions since the end of World War II, that interval averaged about a year and a half. With the Great Depression, however, real GDP took seven years before returning to its 1929 level, according to the new measures of real GDP. Because the labor force kept growing and productivity increasing, unemployment was still high in 1936: 16.9 percent, compared with an estimated 3.2 percent in 1929.

Only the huge rise in demand attributable to World War II eliminated the high unemployment of the 1930s. And, after the war, the economy did not slip back into its pre–World War II condition of high unemployment and idle capacity. Since the war, the economy has enjoyed reasonably full employment, interrupted by recessions of fairly brief duration, and has had mixed experience with inflation.

The comparative mildness of postwar recessions is attributable to many factors. In comparison with the pre–World War II period, government is much more important in the economy. In 1929, total government consumption and investment expenditures were only 14 percent of real GDP. Since 1945, they have never been less than 17 percent. The key point is that government expenditures tend to be independent of business downturns. A similar influence is the growth of government transfer payments, such as Social Security, which continue regardless of business activity and, in the case of the unemployment insurance programs, expand when the economy declines. Transfers in 1998 were 16 percent of personal income; in 1929, only 1.5 percent.

Modern governments with the help of central banks are committed to preventing very severe recessions. Because this policy is widely expected, it tends to limit drastic cuts in private sector spending. By the same token, modern economies may have an inflationary bias.

U.S. CIVILIAN UNEMPLOYMENT RATE, 1929–1998

PERCENT

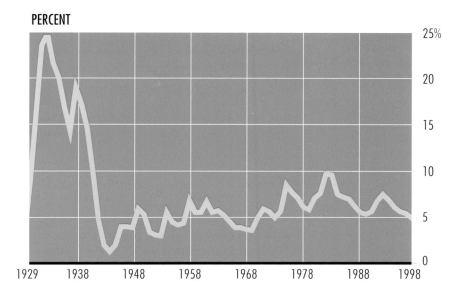

EMPLOYMENT CHANGES IN NONFARM ESTABLISHMENTS DURING ECONOMIC CONTRACTIONS, 1929–1991

PERCENT CHANGE

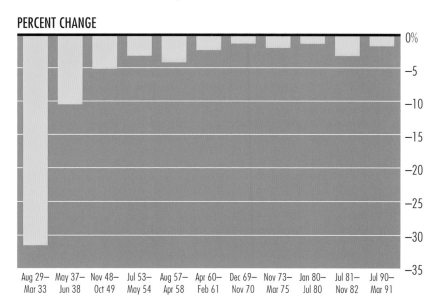

Although the causes of the Great Depression are uncertain, the big decline in the money supply was probably an important factor.

An enormous literature has grown up about the Great Depression and its causes. Although interest in the period had subsided, it picked up again as the twentieth century was drawing to an end.

Many reasons have been given for the depression: the loss of confidence among businessmen and consumers because of the 1929 stock market crash and the bank failures of the early 1930s; the high tariffs passed by Congress in 1930; the "maturing" of the American economy and the decline in investment opportunities; and the perverseness of monetary policy.

Studies made by economists over the postwar years have emphasized the lack of economic understanding on the part of the government, the monetary authorities, and politicians, as well as on the part of economists of the time. President Herbert Hoover was baffled by the economic disaster that beset his administration. In 1932, Franklin D. Roosevelt campaigned on a platform of a balanced budget, but it did not take long for the new administration to step up spending.

Most economists now agree that monetary policy was extremely poor at that time. As a result of the research by economists Milton Friedman and Anna Schwartz, we now know that the Federal Reserve shrank the money supply instead of increasing it as a means of stemming the economic decline. From August 1929 to March 1933, the money stock fell by more than one-third. This was more than three times as much as the largest preceding declines, namely, the reductions of 9 percent in 1875–1879 and again in 1920–1921. Economists now believe that while a severe contraction in economic activity could probably not have been avoided, the economic decline would not have been so pronounced had the money supply not been reduced so much.

U.S. MONEY STOCK, 1913–1939

BILLIONS OF DOLLARS

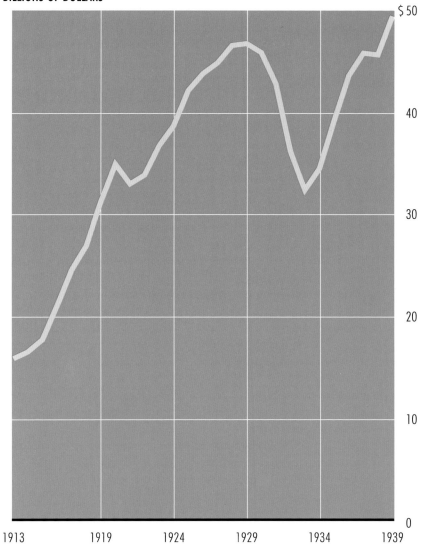

In 1998, 4.5 percent of the civilian labor force was unemployed. Of these workers, about 45 percent had lost their jobs.

The U.S. government uses the Current Population Survey (CPS) to measure unemployment. It has been in existence since 1940, although it has been changed from time to time, with the last major revision in January 1994. The procedures started in 1940 for measuring unemployment were a great step forward. During the 1930s, when unemployment was very high, the public had to contend with several unemployment estimates that differed in both level and movement and were a source of continuing controversy.

The CPS was a genuine breakthrough in two respects: it made use of modern probability sampling methods in a monthly survey on a scale never before seen, and it introduced the concept of the *labor force*. The labor force is the sum of the number of persons employed and the number of persons unemployed; the *unemployment rate* is the number unemployed divided by the labor force. The labor-force concept is a simple one, but even today it is not well understood. Many people think that if employment goes up, unemployment must go down. But that is so only if the labor force is unchanged; experience has demonstrated that the labor force is subject to much change.

To be classified as unemployed in the Current Population Survey, an individual must have had no work in the survey week, must have been available for work, and must have tried to find a job in the four-week period ending in the survey week. In one important breakdown, the survey classifies the unemployed in one of five categories, according to their status at the time they began their job search:

- Job losers. This category includes those who have been given a date to return to work or expect to return to work in six months—persons on temporary layoff—as well as those not having such prospects.
- Persons who completed temporary jobs.
- New entrants—those entering the labor force for the first time.
- Reentrants—those who are coming back to the labor force.
- Job leavers—those who have quit their last job and are looking for another.

The three types of job losers appear on the right in the pie chart.

PERCENTAGE DISTRIBUTION OF UNEMPLOYED, 1998

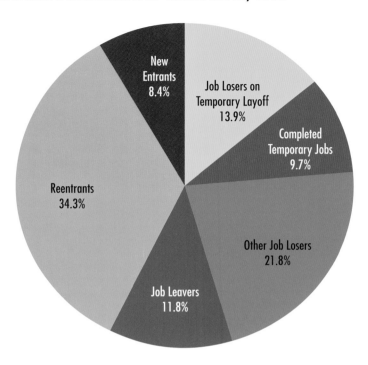

Since the late 1960s, the median duration of unemployment has averaged 6.8 weeks. It was 6.7 weeks in 1998.

Most unemployment is of short duration. Even in 1982, when unemployment was higher than in any other postwar year, 36 percent of the unemployed were out of work for spells of less than 5 weeks. The average (mean) duration of unemployment reached its postwar peak of 20 weeks in 1983, but even then half the unemployed had been out of work for 10 weeks or less (the median duration of unemployment). In 1998, when the average duration was 14.5 weeks, half the unemployed had been out of work for less than 6.7 weeks (the median).

As the chart indicates, the mean length of unemployment has increased over the postwar years. One aspect of this is the proportion of the unemployed who have experienced very long spells of unemployment. In the 1950s, less than 10 percent of the unemployed had spells lasting more than six months, but in the years 1990–1998, the proportion rose to 16.5 percent. This sharp increase in the long-term proportion is probably related to structural changes in the economy, such as the one associated with the oil shock of 1973; to cutbacks in defense production associated with the end of the cold war; and to attempts by business to reduce costs under conditions of heightened competition.

The duration statistics themselves are subject to two biases that operate in different directions. As a random sample of households, they are more likely to pick an individual who has had a long period of unemployment than a person who was unemployed only briefly, say, a few weeks. In contrast, a person who reports that he has been unemployed for a given number of weeks is describing a condition that has not been completed.

DURATION OF UNEMPLOYMENT, IN WEEKS, 1948–1998

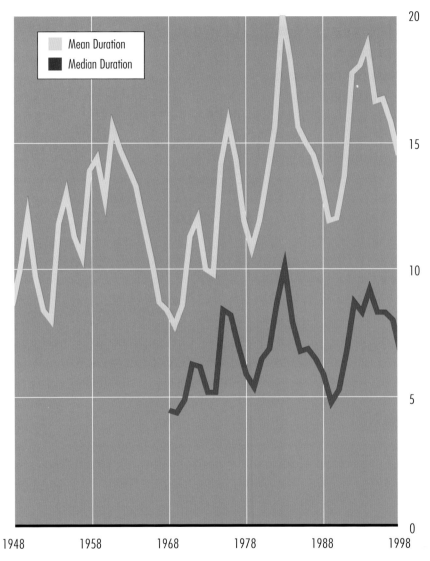

Note: Data for the median are not available before 1968.

Unemployment rates for persons with white-collar jobs are typically much lower than for those with blue-collar jobs.

Throughout American history, the introduction of labor-saving technologies has been accompanied by deep concern that the new technology would bring about a large rise in unemployment. The record since 1940, when official unemployment measures started, does show a rise in the civilian unemployment rate, but it is by no means clear that this is a consequence of technological change. Estimates of unemployment for the twentieth century before 1940 made by Stanley Lebergott portray a rather flat picture (by decades) until the Great Depression.

The 1960s saw great concern over automation, which was the first application of computer technology to industrial processes. There can be little doubt that, throughout the post–World War II period, the introduction of all kinds of labor-saving devices has held down the demand for blue-collar workers. At its peak in 1979, employment of production workers in manufacturing—the blue-collar core of factory employees—was only one-sixth higher than in 1948; employment of all other workers in manufacturing more than doubled over the same period, and all private nonfarm employment was 88 percent higher. The 1980s were especially difficult for factory labor, with employment down and blue-collar unemployment rates sharply higher. Blue-collar unemployment rates associated with the 1990–1992 recession, however, were not nearly as high as in 1982 and 1983, whereas white-collar unemployment rates were only moderately lower.

White-collar unemployment rates have always been much lower than blue-collar rates. Both types rose from the 1960s to the 1970s to the 1980s, but a difference has shown up in the 1990s (through 1998). On average, white-collar rates in the 1990s are only a little lower than those in the 1980s, whereas blue-collar rates are much lower. Defense cutbacks and restructuring by large companies have held down the employment growth of lower-paid white-collar workers but have not prevented a large expansion in the employment of managerial and professional workers. In addition, the sustained expansion in the economy since the early part of the 1990s has kept blue-collar unemployment rates relatively low.

UNEMPLOYMENT RATES IN BLUE- AND WHITE-COLLAR OCCUPATIONS, 1958–1998

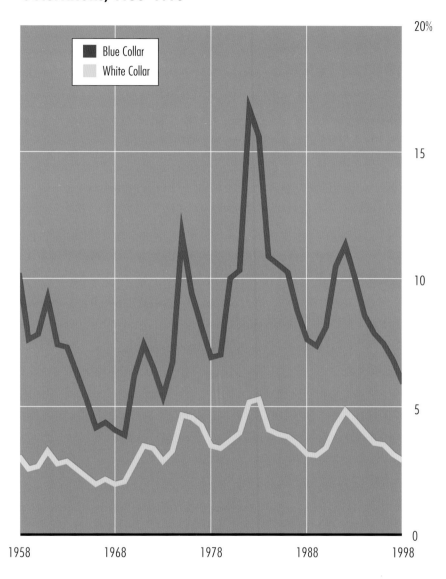

Legend:
- Blue Collar
- White Collar

A fairly large proportion of the labor force experiences some unemployment during any year.

The results of the monthly unemployment survey have been likened to a snapshot. The snapshot records, for the survey week of each month, persons working and persons looking for work. Those who had looked for work but had decided to stop in the survey week and those who had intended to seek work at a later date but had not begun their search as of the survey week do not appear in the labor force statistics of that month. Generally speaking, only those who were working or were still looking for work are counted as part of the labor force. Ordinarily, persons who did not seek work in the survey week are excluded from the labor force.

Brief spells of unemployment are fairly common in the U.S. labor market. In 1997, when the official unemployment rate was 4.9 percent, persons who had experienced some unemployment were 10.8 percent of the number of persons who had either worked or looked for work that year. (Persons who either worked or looked for work at any time during the year typically constitute a somewhat larger number than the civilian labor force. These figures, obtained once each year, come from the survey of "work experience" conducted by the Bureau of Labor Statistics; the latest available numbers are those for 1997.) Of those with some unemployment at any time in 1997, 86 percent worked at some point during that year.

PERCENTAGE OF PERSONS WITH SOME UNEMPLOYMENT AND THE OFFICIAL UNEMPLOYMENT RATE, 1958–1998

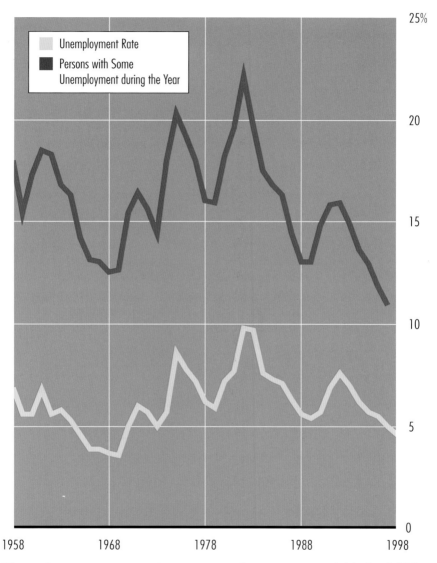

Note: Data on persons with some unemployment not available for 1998.

The rate of unemployment consistent with "high" employment rose during the 1950s, 1960s, and 1970s, but declined thereafter.

Even under the best of conditions, some unemployment is inevitable, as some workers are between jobs or just entering the labor force or are in disagreement with potential employers about terms of employment. Economists have tried to define and measure what is sometimes called the *natural rate of unemployment*, or the nonaccelerating inflation rate of unemployment (NAIRU), meaning the rate at which there would be no tendency for the rate of inflation to increase. We show here one such measurement, the NAIRU as calculated by the Congressional Budget Office. The increase up to 1977 was partly because of the increase in the proportion of women and young people in the labor force, since a large number of them were new entrants or reentrants seeking employment. Also, the experience of rising inflation and low unemployment during the 1960s and early 1970s generated expectations of more inflation and of wage increases to compensate. Such anticipation made it difficult to stabilize the inflation rate without more unemployment than had been necessary at an earlier time. The experience of the 1980s and 1990s changed these expectations and made a lower rate of unemployment consistent with lower and more stable inflation.

HIGH-EMPLOYMENT UNEMPLOYMENT AND THE ACTUAL UNEMPLOYMENT RATE, 1950–1998

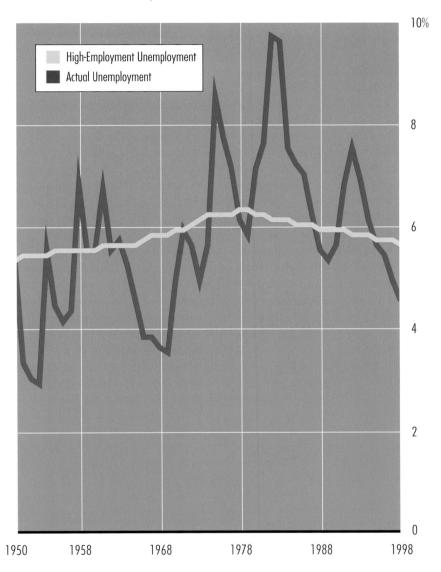

For several years, the unemployment rate in the United States has been lower than rates in other major countries.

In recent years, unemployment rates in the major industrialized countries—except Japan–have been much higher than in this country. In 1998, for example, when the U.S. rate was 4.5 percent, rates were 12 percent in France and Italy and 8 percent in Canada. This was not always the case. In the ten years from 1974 to 1983, which embraced the two oil shocks, the U.S. unemployment rate was above that of the other major member-countries of the Organization for Economic Cooperation and Development (OECD), except Canada. From 1989 to 1998, however, the U.S. rate fell, while rates abroad rose (see chart). Japan's low unemployment rate, even after the rise during the 1990s, is probably a reflection of definitions that differ from those in North America and Western Europe.

The usual explanation for the changed unemployment situation concerns differences in labor markets. Whereas the United States has relatively free markets in which business and labor can move with ease, businesses in foreign countries are hampered by high wages and restrictive labor practices. This country once led all others in wages paid in manufacturing, but that has not been true for some time. Social benefits abroad are maintained at a high level, as are the taxes required to finance them.

The operation of product markets may provide another explanation. Businesses abroad are often hampered by restrictive regulations that make innovations difficult. For example, many European countries limit by law the hours during which retail stores may operate; as a consequence, large-scale, lower-cost retail operations are discouraged.

European integration is attempting to modify restrictive practices of all kinds, but the imposition of uniform standards may make adjustments more difficult to bring about. Countries may find it hard to make the choices about wages, working conditions, and social benefits, as well as about the working of product markets, that will avoid higher unemployment.

UNEMPLOYMENT RATES BY COUNTRY, 1974–1983 AND 1989–1998

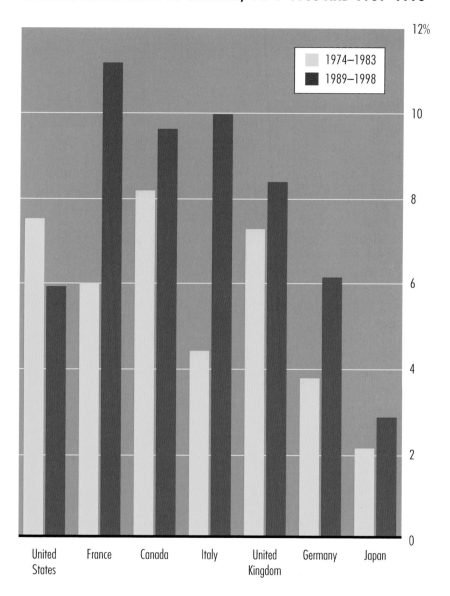

Legend:
- 1974–1983
- 1989–1998

Before World War II, inflation was unusual in the United States, except in wartime. Since World War II, inflation has continued, even in peacetime.

There is common, though not unanimous, agreement that the official consumer price index overstates the rate of inflation in recent years, for reasons explained in the "Introduction" and on page 252. However, no superior historical series has been calculated. The figures charted here cannot be taken as precisely measuring the true rate of inflation—something that is probably not measurable anyway—but they are probably a valid representation of the big swings in the rate of inflation in our history.

The rate of inflation surged during the wars of the past 137 years. After the Civil War and World War I, the United States entered prolonged periods in which the price level fluctuated around a declining trend, and most of the wartime inflation was erased. That did not happen after World War II, the Korean War, or the 1970s experience, which combined the inflationary effects of the Vietnam War with the two oil shocks. Even in the relatively calm period from 1982 to 1996, the consumer price index, as officially calculated, rose by 3.5 percent a year. If, as some have suggested, the official figures overstate the true rate of inflation by 1 percent a year, that rate was 2.5 percent a year, a rate that would double the price level in 30 years. This is much higher than the measured rate from 1860 to 1916, which includes the Civil War, and much higher than the measured rate from 1916 to 1940, which includes World War I.

One reason for the difference in price behavior between the periods before and after 1940 may have been the increased commitment of the government after the depression of the 1930s to use all its powers to keep unemployment low, so that government policy became expansionary whenever unemployment threatened to rise.

In 1997 and 1998, the inflation rate as officially measured averaged 1.9 percent. In those years, a different policy, placing more emphasis on price-level stability, may have been the main reason why inflation and unemployment were both lower than had been experienced earlier.

FIVE-YEAR AVERAGE OF YEAR-TO-YEAR PERCENTAGE CHANGES IN CONSUMER PRICES, 1860–1998

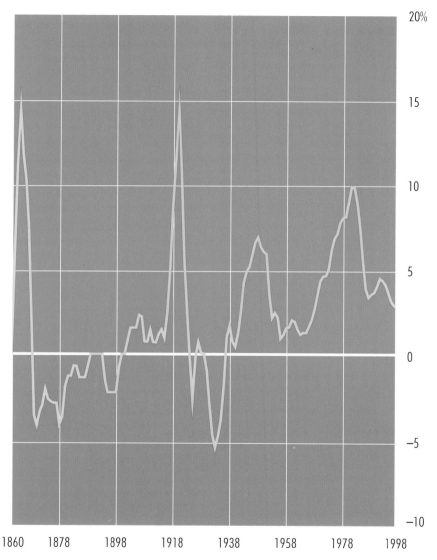

Note: Data are five-year moving averages centered on the last year.

Management of monetary policy in the short run encounters many difficulties.

The difficulty of managing monetary policy arises mainly in connection with the ordinary fluctuations of output and the price level. The chart illustrates both the possibilities and the difficulties of stabilizing the economy by the use of monetary policy. (The chart compares the rate of increase in the money supply with the change in the price index two years later.) During most of the period shown, there was a rough correspondence in the direction of change in the rate of increase of the money supply and the subsequent rate of increase of the price level. There was, however, a large variation in the two rates of increase. During most of the time, the money supply was increasing faster than the price level, but, from 1978 to 1980 and from 1993 to 1995, the opposite was true. Also, in the early part of the period and again after 1987, the two variables often moved in different directions. In the late 1990s, there were several years of fairly stable and low inflation. This brief experience still left uncertain the ability of monetary policy to stabilize the economy or the price level within narrow limits.

Various strategies have been proposed for managing monetary policy in the face of its short-run uncertainties:

- stabilization of a particular price, usually the price of gold
- stabilization of the rate of growth of the money supply, somehow defined
- "feed-back" rules that would make the money supply respond automatically and promptly to observed changes in economic conditions
- discretionary adjustment of the money supply to the state of the economy as appraised by the Federal Reserve
- discretionary adjustment of interest rates

On the whole, monetary authorities have preferred discretionary strategies. At the end of 1998, the dominant strategy of the Federal Reserve seemed to be to decide from time to time on the short-term interest rate that it thought most likely to yield the desired behavior of the economy.

THREE-YEAR CHANGES IN MONEY AND PRICES, 1962–1996

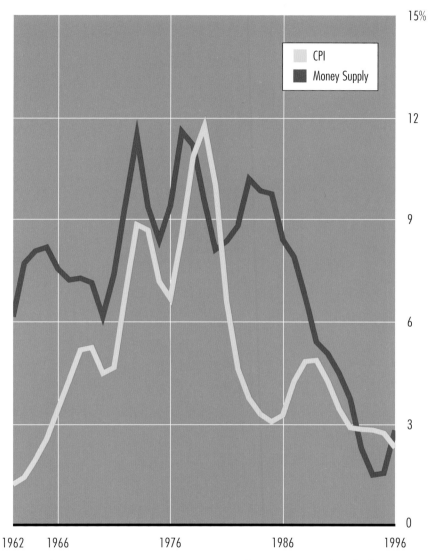

Note: Three-year increase in money supply is compared with three-year increase of CPI two years later.

PART THIRTEEN

Government Expenditures, Taxes, and Deficits

Total government expenditures, relative to GDP, are now more than three times as high as they were before the Great Depression.

The charts refer to the total of federal, state, and local expenditures and include transfer payments and interest, as well as purchases of goods and services. Most of the rise in the ratio (bottom chart) occurred by 1949, when it was already about 2.2 times as high as in 1929. The increase during this period—excluding the years of World War II and the Korean War—resulted from the programs introduced during the New Deal and from the residue of World War II, including interest on the war debt, benefits to veterans, and the higher level of peacetime defense spending.

After 1949, the ratio of government spending to GDP was on a slowly rising trend, from about 25 percent to about 35 percent, punctuated by upticks during the Korean War, the Vietnam War, and the occasional recession. This upward trend resulted primarily from rising transfer payments, including, notably, Social Security benefits. At the end of the 1990s, there are signs that the ratio has stabilized, and may be declining, because of the decline in defense spending after the end of the cold war and the decline of interest burdens as interest rates fell.

TOTAL GOVERNMENT EXPENDITURES BASED ON CHAINED 1992 DOLLARS, 1929–1998

INDEXES: 1929=100

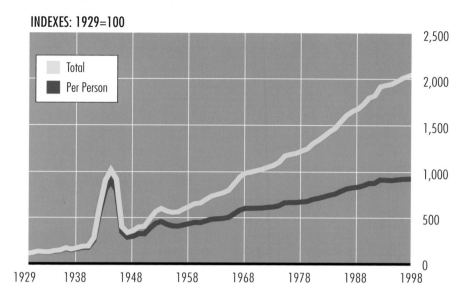

TOTAL GOVERNMENT EXPENDITURES AS PERCENTAGE OF GDP, 1929–1998

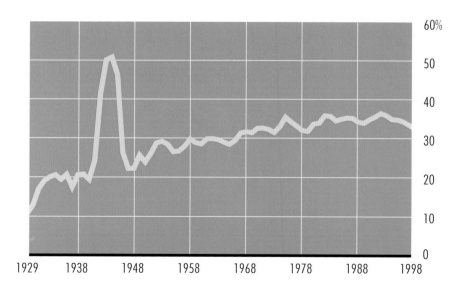

Real federal expenditures in 1998 were 6.5 times as high as in 1948.

Real federal expenditures in 1948, while much higher than before World War II, were at a low point after the wartime buildup. Over the next fifty years, expenditures increased at an annual average rate of 3.8 percent. The pace of increase was, however, quite uneven. There were three intervals, 1953–1965, 1968–1974, and 1990–1998, when the annual rate of increase was less than 1 percent. In each of these periods, defense spending was declining after large increases associated with the Korean and Vietnam Wars and the Reagan defense buildup. The period 1990–1998 was unusual in that there were both a decline in defense spending and a rise in nondefense spending that was well below its postwar average.

The long stretch from 1974 to 1990, in which the rise of total expenditures was at just about its postwar average rate, can be divided into two parts. In the first, from 1974 to 1981, total spending rose at more than the average rate, but defense spending rose little, and nondefense spending rose at much more than the average rate. In the second, from 1981 to 1990, the period of the Reagan defense buildup, total spending rose at less than the average rate, despite an above-average rate of increase in defense spending.

By 1998, real federal spending per capita was 3.5 times as high as it had been in 1948. Per capita nondefense spending was 4.7 times as high as it had been. Most of this increase was in transfer payments, such as Social Security and Medicare, as shown in following pages.

FEDERAL GOVERNMENT OUTLAYS, 1948–1998

BASED ON CHAINED 1992 DOLLARS; INDEX: 1948=100

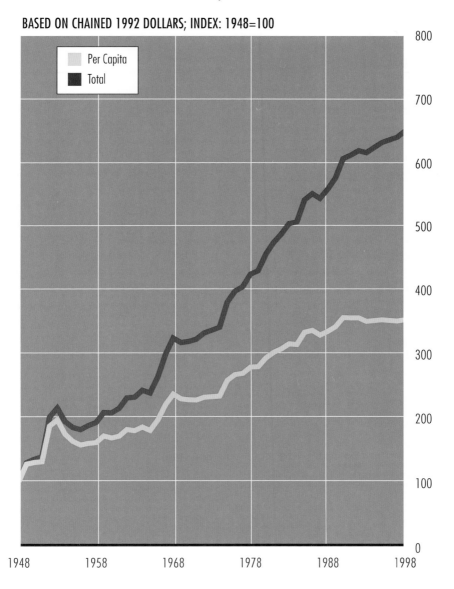

Before the Great Depression, state and local expenditures were much larger than federal expenditures, but, since 1939, that situation has been reversed.

In 1929, state and local expenditures were about three times as large as federal expenditures. During the New Deal, the relative size of the federal government grew, as it assumed responsibility for relief and recovery from the depression. This was also the time of some buildup of defense spending, which, though tiny by our later experience, was still large relative to the budgets of that period.

The dominance of the federal sector since World War II is attributable in part to the expansion of expenditures for functions that have always been federal, mainly defense and interest on the federal debt. But this change has also been a consequence of the rapid growth of federal expenditures in fields that the federal government did not formerly occupy, notably, Social Security and health care.

Part of the expenditures made by state and local governments are financed by grants from the federal government. If these are considered expenditures of the federal government, the federal share of total government expenditures is about 66 percent; if they are considered state and local expenditures, the federal share is about 58 percent.

The federal share declined significantly from its peak of 92 percent (including grants) to its 66 percent share in 1998. This drop resulted primarily from the decline in defense spending but was partly the result of a slowdown in the growth of other federal spending.

The federal lead is in transfer payments and interest. State and local expenditures of other kinds are much higher than federal expenditures. The number of state and local employees is about 3.2 times the number of federal employees, including the armed forces.

Although total state and local expenditures have declined markedly relative to federal expenditures, they remain about as high relative to GDP as they were in 1929—about 11 percent if only expenditures from their own resources are counted.

FEDERAL EXPENDITURES AS PERCENTAGE OF TOTAL FEDERAL, STATE, AND LOCAL EXPENDITURES, 1929–1998

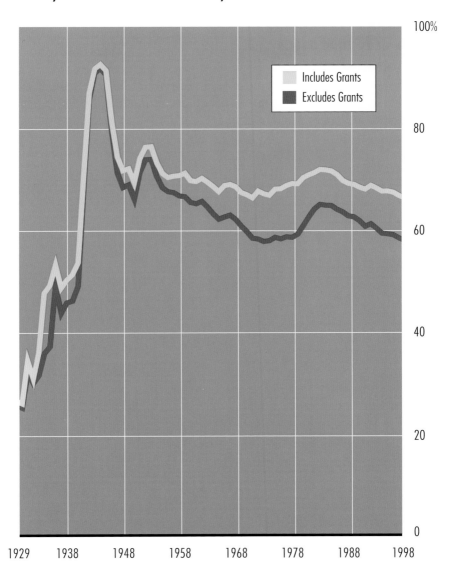

Defense spending as a percentage of GDP was lower in 1998 than in any other year since the 1920s.

At the height of World War II, defense spending was about 38 percent of GDP. In the postwar demobilization, it fell to less than 4 percent. With the Korean War, the ratio surged to 14 percent. Since then, with brief interruptions for the Vietnam War and the defense buildup of the 1980s, defense spending has fallen to less than 3.5 percent. Measurement of the amount of real defense spending is difficult, but it is probably not far from what it was in the interlude between World War II and the Korean War.

DEFENSE SPENDING AS PERCENTAGE OF GDP, 1947–1998

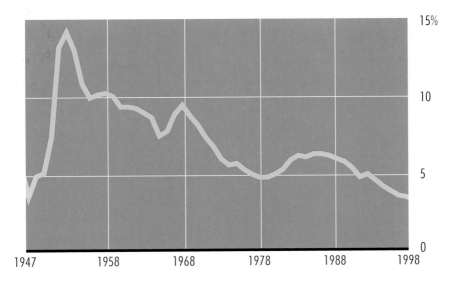

DEFENSE SPENDING, 1947–1998

BILLIONS OF 1992 DOLLARS

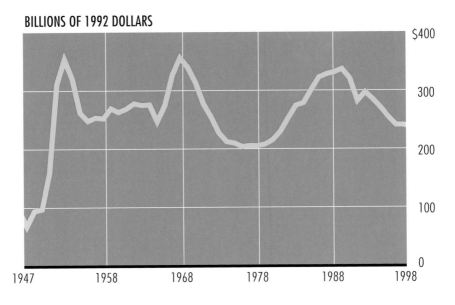

The rise of nondefense spending has been dominated by expenditures for health, income support, and education.

Between 1952 and 1997, total government nondefense expenditures (federal, state, and local) doubled as a share of GDP, from 14 percent to 29 percent. About 80 percent of that increase went to three main functions: health, income support, and education. Expenditures for these functions rose from 50 percent of total nondefense expenditures to 65 percent. The great increases in health and income support were at the federal level. All the increase in expenditures for education, as a share of GDP, was at the state and local levels, where it doubled from 2.7 to 5.4 percent of GDP.

The increase for health was primarily caused by Medicare, although Medicaid was also a significant factor. The increase for income support was primarily for Social Security. These two categories, health and income support, accounted for more than 80 percent of the increase in federal expenditures as a share of GDP. Together with interest, they account for all the increase in the federal nondefense share.

Interest expenditures more than doubled as a share of GDP, all at the federal level, as a result of the increase in the federal debt and in rates of interest.

Expenditures for all functions other than those mentioned above, which include public safety, roads and other transportation facilities, and the operation of the government, rose from 5.9 to 7.4 percent of GDP.

FEDERAL, STATE, AND LOCAL NONDEFENSE EXPENDITURES, BY MAJOR PURPOSE, AS PERCENTAGES OF GDP, 1952 AND 1997

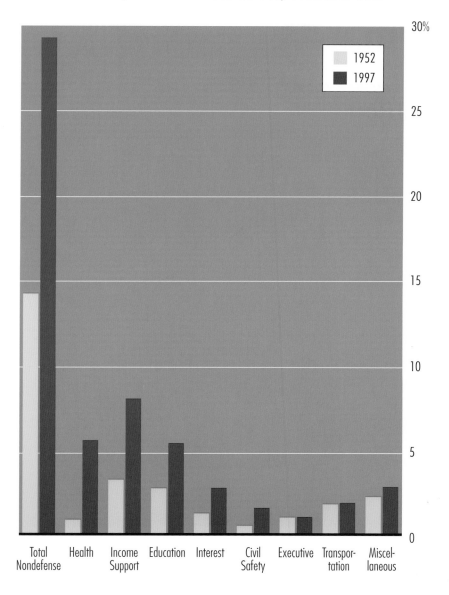

Federal payments directed specifically to low-income persons have risen substantially in the past decades and are now about 2.2 percent of GDP.

By 1998, federal payments to individuals had risen to 57 percent of total outlays, from 32 percent in 1962. This category of outlays consists of transfer payments and does not include payments in exchange for goods or services provided or money lent to the government (interest). Payments to individuals constituted 82 percent of all federal outlays other than those for national defense or interest. This allocation of outlays reveals a government whose main function, except for defense, is shifting money around from taxpayers to various beneficiaries, most of whom are also taxpayers, or have been.

Between 1962 and 1998, federal payments to individuals rose from 6.1 percent of GDP to 11.2 percent. (The ratio peaked at 12.0 percent in 1991.) In 1998, about 63 percent of these payments were for Social Security and Medicare. Payments under these programs had increased greatly because of the burgeoning beneficiary population—mainly the aged—and expanded benefits mandated by legislative changes, higher earnings of retiring workers, and higher medical costs. Large additional amounts went for the retirement benefits of federal workers and for veterans.

Federal payments to people eligible for benefits only because they are poor—"means-tested" benefits—rose from less than 1 percent of GDP to about 2.2 percent between 1962 and 1998. This amount consisted mainly of payments under the Medicaid, food stamp, and public assistance programs. In 1998, they constituted about 13 percent of total federal outlays.

FEDERAL PAYMENTS TO INDIVIDUALS AS PERCENTAGES OF GDP, 1962–1998

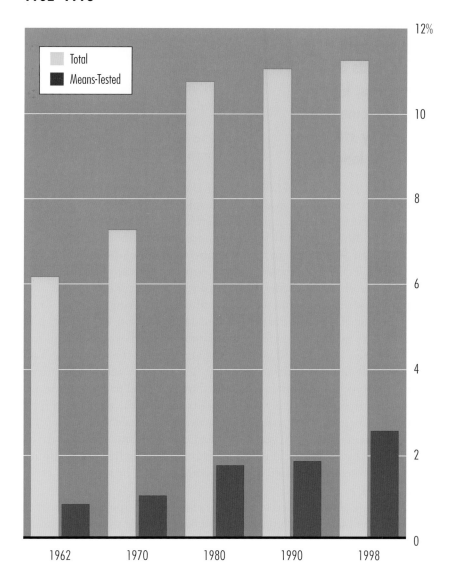

The ratio of benefits received under Social Security to the taxes paid by any individual depends on his earnings, his time of retirement, his family status, and his longevity.

When the Social Security system was established in 1935, it was clear that the first retirees would have few years of employment on which Social Security taxes had been paid. To provide them with what were considered adequate retirement benefits, the system was arranged so that the ratio of benefits to covered earnings would be higher for people with low covered earnings than for those with higher covered earnings. As time passed, Social Security taxes and benefits were raised, and the higher benefits were made available to people who had formerly paid taxes at the lower rates. Thus, those people who retired in the first years of the program and those who earned lower incomes received much more benefit relative to their payments into their accounts than those who have retired or will retire subsequently or those who have earned or will earn higher incomes.

The upper chart shows the number of years of receiving benefits after retiring at age sixty-five that would be required for a single worker to recover the Social Security taxes that had been paid on his behalf, plus interest. (The calculations refer to the combined employer and employee taxes and to an estimated share of those taxes that is for the worker's retirement and not for benefits to survivors, and assume a future real interest rate of 2.8 percent.) A worker who retired in 1998 and had always earned the minimum wage would get back benefits equal to the taxes paid on his behalf in 10.6 years. If he had always earned the average wage of covered workers, it would take 15.5 years; if he had earned the maximum wage on which tax was paid, it would take 21.3 years. These figures were all much lower for workers who retired in earlier years and will be much higher for those retiring in the future.

Benefits are also provided for spouses of retirees. A spouse not entitled to benefits on his own earnings receives a benefit equal to half that of the covered worker. The lower chart shows the years required for such a couple to recover the taxes paid. The number of years is significantly smaller than for the single worker.

These calculations are sensitive to the rate of interest that will be earned on Social Security reserves. The higher that rate is, the longer it will take for the retired worker to recover the taxes paid on his behalf, plus interest.

YEARS FOR SINGLE WORKER TO RECOVER RETIREMENT PORTION OF COMBINED TAXES, 1960, 1998, AND 2030

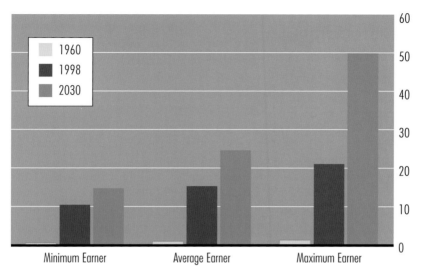

Note: Date indicates year of retirement.

YEARS FOR WORKER WITH A DEPENDENT SPOUSE TO RECOVER RETIREMENT PORTION OF COMBINED TAXES, 1960, 1998, AND 2030

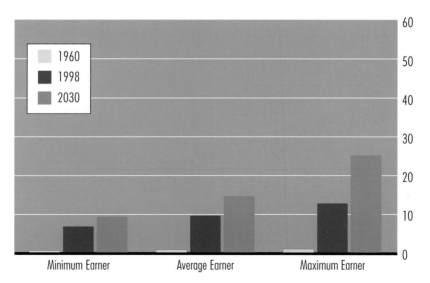

Note: Date indicates year of retirement.

Since the early 1950s, federal employment has declined substantially as a fraction of total employment.

The number of its employees is one measure of the federal government's role in the economy and in society. Although the path of federal employment shows bulges during the Korean War and the Vietnam War, its declining trend relative to total employment is clear. The absolute number of employees has declined from 7.6 million in 1968, during the Vietnam War, to 5.3 million in 1997. Almost all that decline was in the armed forces. Civilian employment has fluctuated in a narrow range and is now just about as high as it was thirty years ago. Since then, civilian employment in the Department of Defense has declined substantially, so that employment outside the Department of Defense, which was about 1.7 million in 1968, is now about 2.2 million. But because that expansion has not kept up with the growth of the total work force, federal employment is now about 3.7 percent of total employment, compared with 8.9 percent in 1968.

Real federal expenditures per employee were four times as high in 1997 as in 1950. The rise of federal expenditures since 1950, aside from the war intervals, was concentrated in programs that used relatively few people to pay out large amounts of money. Expenditures for Social Security, Medicare, and interest are leading examples. Expenditures per employee in the Departments of Health and Human Services and of Education and in the Social Security Administration, combined, are about seven times as high as in the Department of Defense.

FEDERAL EMPLOYMENT AS PERCENTAGE OF TOTAL EMPLOYMENT, 1950–1997

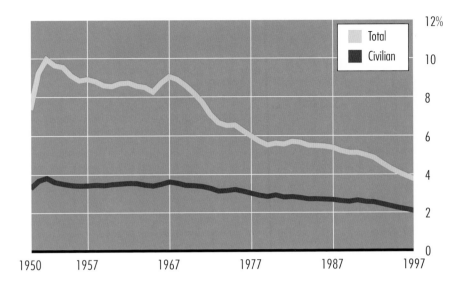

TOTAL AND CIVILIAN FEDERAL EMPLOYEES, 1950–1997

THOUSANDS OF EMPLOYEES

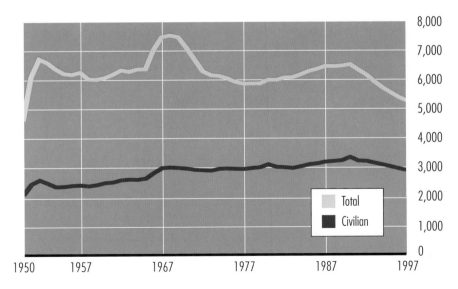

Total federal revenues have fluctuated within a narrow range since 1960, as the increase in payroll taxes has offset the decline of all other taxes combined.

At their peak in World War II, federal taxes were about 21 percent of GDP. Tax cuts after the war reduced the ratio below 15 percent, but soon the ratio returned to 17–19 percent. Since 1960, the ratio has never dipped below 17 percent but has exceeded 19 percent in only seven years. In 1998, at 20.5, the ratio topped 20 percent for the first time since World War II.

The ratio rose slightly above 19 percent in fiscal years 1969 and 1970, with a temporary surtax to help finance the Vietnam War. It then declined when the surtax expired. The ratio began to rise after 1978, as inflation pushed income-tax payers into higher brackets. The 1981 tax cut undid that increase. The ratio rose after 1993, because economic growth again raised taxpayers into higher brackets and because corporate profits rose.

Although the ratio of total revenue to GDP has fluctuated within a narrow range, the composition of the revenue has changed substantially. The major alteration was the rise of the payroll tax. Receipts from payroll taxes rose from 2.8 percent of GDP in 1960 to 6.8 percent in 1998. Social Security payroll tax rates were raised, the ceiling on wages subject to tax was increased, coverage was expanded, and a new tax for Medicare was imposed in 1966.

Aside from payroll taxes, receipts from all other taxes declined as a share of GDP, from 15 percent in 1960 to 13 percent in 1997, before rising in 1998 to 13.7 percent. The decline occurred primarily because of the decline in corporate taxes, from 4.1 percent of GDP in 1960 to 1.1 percent in 1983, before an increase to 2.2 percent in 1998. Book profits of corporations, relative to GDP, were lower in 1998 than in 1960, and the effective rate of taxation on corporate profits was also lower.

Individual income-tax receipts showed no clear trend; since 1960, they have never been below 7 percent of GDP and rarely been above 9 percent. Although income-tax rates were reduced from time to time, these reductions mainly offset the rise of income-tax burdens from the interaction of economic growth and inflation with a progressive tax rate structure. Since 1981, individual income-tax brackets have been raised annually in proportion to the price level; this modification eliminated the increase of the individual tax burden from inflation. The effect of real growth remains.

In 1998, individual income-tax receipts rose to 9.9 percent of GDP, exceeding the highest ratios of World War II. This increase may have resulted from the steep rise of stock prices during 1997.

FEDERAL REVENUES AS PERCENTAGE OF GDP, 1948–1998

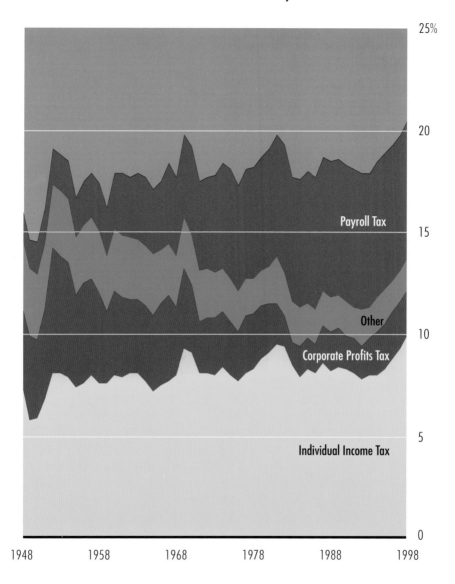

25%

20

Payroll Tax

15

Other

10

Corporate Profits Tax

5

Individual Income Tax

0

1948   1958   1968   1978   1988   1998

Federal income taxes were a little lower in 1996 than in 1985 for families at a wide range of income levels, and much lower for those qualifying for the earned-income credit.

In 1985, a married couple with two dependents and an income of $35,000 (in 1995 dollars) would have paid a federal income tax of 9.6 percent of its income. In 1990, the same couple, with the same real income, would have paid 8.2 percent, and, by 1997, the rate had fallen a little further, to 7.8 percent. The same family, with an income of $75,000 (in 1995 dollars), would have paid 18.1 percent in 1985, 15.1 percent in 1990, and 14.6 percent in 1997. For these families, the marginal tax rate—the percentage of an additional dollar of income that would be paid in tax—declined between 1985 and 1990 but remained unchanged from 1990 to 1997.

The taxation of the lowest-income families, however, changed dramatically as a result of the increase of the earned-income tax credit. (Under the EITC, low-income earners receive a credit that is larger the lower their income and the higher the number of their children. The credit is deducted from income tax and refunded in cash to the extent that it exceeds income tax due.) In 1985, a family with an income of $10,000 (in 1995 dollars) would have received a tax refund, that is, "paid" a negative tax, equal to 8.1 percent of its income. By 1990, the refund had increased to 11 percent, and, by 1997, it had jumped to 34 percent. In 1985, that family's refund would have declined by 12.2 percent of a dollar of additional earned income. That was its marginal rate. In 1990 and 1996, earning an additional dollar of income would not have reduced the refund at all. It was in a range of the earned-income zone where the refund was constant. At a little higher level of earned income, the credit began to phase out and was reduced by 20 percent of additional earnings.

(These calculations refer to families that have one earner, all of whose income is taxable, and take the standard deductions. The results would differ somewhat for families in different circumstances.)

AVERAGE FEDERAL INCOME TAX RATE AS PERCENTAGE OF INCOME, 1985, 1990, AND 1997

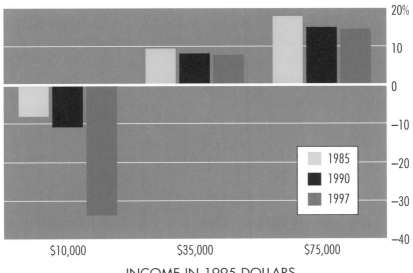

INCOME IN 1995 DOLLARS

MARGINAL FEDERAL INCOME TAX RATE AS PERCENTAGE OF ADDITIONAL INCOME, 1985, 1990, AND 1997

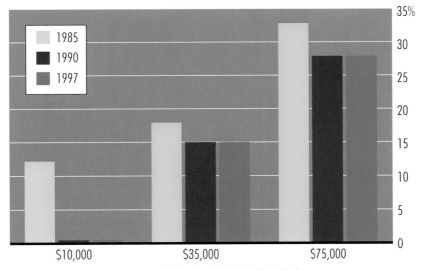

INCOME IN 1995 DOLLARS

Note: Marginal tax rate for $10,000 class was zero in 1990 and 1996.

Total government expenditures and receipts as a percentage of GDP are low in the United States compared with other industrial countries.

In 1997, both government receipts and government expenditures, relative to GDP, were lower than in any European industrial country. In Japan, expenditures were higher, but receipts were at the same level as in the United States. Only in Korea were receipts and expenditures, relative to GDP, lower than in the United States.

The ratio of both expenditures and receipts to GDP has risen over the period shown here, and probably for much longer, in all countries. The rise has been less in the United States than in other countries, because defense spending was much larger here and its decline has had a more significant impact on the budget.

The figures shown here probably overestimate somewhat the excess of Europe over the United States in the amount of spending due to government policies. In the United States, some expenditures, especially for health, are stimulated by government tax advantages, which do not appear in the government budget but are considered private expenditures; in many European countries, such expenditures are made directly by governments and appear in their budgets. But even when allowance is made for this fact, government-induced expenditures are higher in Europe.

GOVERNMENT RECEIPTS AS PERCENTAGE OF GDP, BY AREA, 1968, 1978, AND 1997

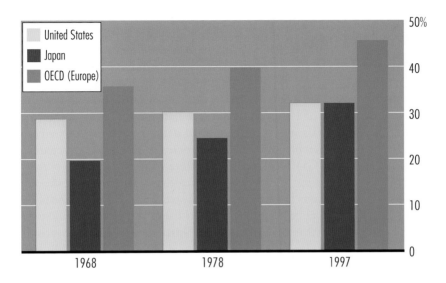

GOVERNMENT EXPENDITURES AS PERCENTAGE OF GDP, BY AREA, 1968, 1978, AND 1997

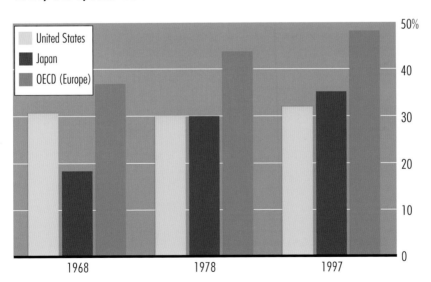

During most of our history, significant deficits in the federal budget have resulted only from wars or recessions.

World War II and the depression of the 1930s stand out as sources of deficits. Aside from those events and the recession of 1974–1975, deficits, though common, never exceeded 3 percent of GDP until the 1980s. The defense buildup of the 1980s, the recession of 1981–1982, and the tax cut of 1981 introduced a period of thirteen years in which the annual deficits averaged 4.2 percent of GDP. These deficits persisted even after defense expenditures began to decline as a share of GDP, because that decline was offset in large part by rises in expenditures for Social Security, health, and interest on the national debt. The deficits began to decline, however, in the mid-1990s; by fiscal 1998, the budget came into surplus. If the tax and expenditure programs existing in 1998 remain in force, surpluses are expected to continue for another ten years, barring a recession. Even without the possibility of a recession, the outlook—depending heavily on the rate of economic growth and the trend of health costs, among other things—is uncertain.

(These figures show the conventional measurement of the deficit and the surplus. Alternative measurements are shown on page 237. Those measurements show substantially different sizes of the deficit, or surplus, but would not significantly change the historical trend.)

FEDERAL EXPENDITURES, RECEIPTS, AND DEFICITS AS PERCENTAGES OF GDP, 1929–1998

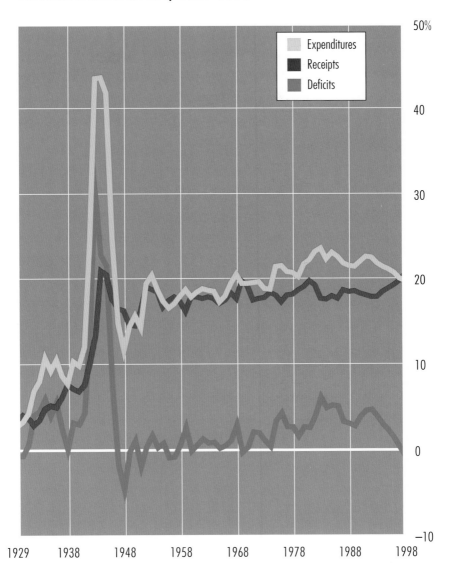

The rise of the federal debt, relative to GDP, since the early 1970s stopped in the 1990s.

The federal debt rose enormously during World War II and reached a level exceeding GDP. Although the debt continued to increase because of budget deficits, the ratio of the debt to GDP fell sharply. Between the end of 1946 and the end of 1974, the absolute size of the debt rose by more than 42 percent, but as a percentage of GDP, it fell from 109 percent to 24 percent. That decline was attributable to the strong rise of GDP, partly resulting from inflation. During that period, the real value of the debt—the debt adjusted for the rise of the consumer price index—fell by almost 44 percent.

After 1974, the ratio of the debt to GDP began to rise, as the size of deficits relative to GDP rose. But for several years beginning in 1993, the ratio stabilized at 50 percent, and, since 1996, it has declined slightly, as the size of deficits fell.

The interest burden—the ratio of federal interest to GDP—fell after World War II but fell less rapidly than the debt-to-GDP ratio; after 1974, it rose more rapidly than the debt-to-GDP ratio. This movement of the interest burden relative to the debt burden reflected the rise of the interest rates on the outstanding debt, as market interest rates rose and as the World War II debt, which had been incurred at extremely low rates, had to be refinanced at higher rates. But the interest burden stabilized around 1984, as interest rates subsided from the extraordinary peaks reached around 1980, and the burden has since declined as deficits fell.

The figures shown here refer to the debt held by the public and the interest on that debt. It excludes debt held by federal government accounts, mainly the Social Security Trust Fund. The general pattern shown in the charts would also be true of the total debt, except that its level would be higher and its increase over the entire period would be greater.

The government has a large and growing obligation to pay benefits to present and future beneficiaries of Social Security. This obligation is not measured by the debt of the government held by the trust fund. If this obligation is considered part of the government's "debt," even though not represented by Treasury securities, the debt is much larger and still rising.

FEDERAL DEBT HELD BY PUBLIC AS PERCENTAGE OF GDP, 1940–1998

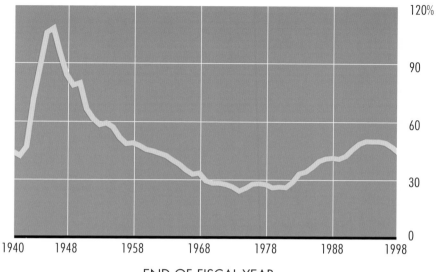

END OF FISCAL YEAR

FEDERAL NET INTEREST AS PERCENTAGE OF GDP, 1940–1998

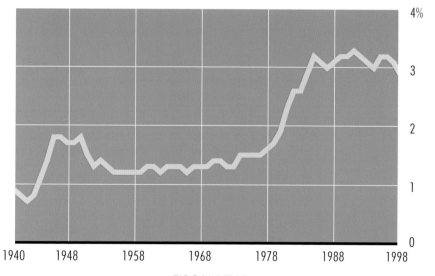

FISCAL YEAR

Fluctuations in the economy increase fluctuations in the deficit or the surplus.

A rise of the economy, with increasing incomes, raises the tax base and raises the revenue if tax rates are unchanged. Expenditures for unemployment compensation and some other expenditures tied to earnings or unemployment also decline. Thus, the deficit declines or the surplus rises as the economy rises, and the opposite happens as the economy falls.

This response of the budget to cyclical changes in the economy is commonly considered an *automatic stabilizer*, tending to limit the size of economic fluctuations. When the economy declines and incomes fall, private after-tax incomes fall less than they otherwise would, because some decline in incomes is absorbed by a decline in taxes. In addition, part of the loss of private incomes is made up by unemployment compensation and other government payments. The net effect is to limit the decline in private spending.

This stabilizing effect is called *automatic*, because it occurs without any decision by government to change tax or expenditure programs. While the power of the automatic stabilizing effect is uncertain, it seems clearly desirable, in appraising fiscal policy, to distinguish changes in the deficit or surplus attributable to cyclical, temporary economic fluctuations from those attributable to other causes.

The chart shows the actual deficit, as a percentage of GDP, and an estimated deficit in each year had the economy been at high employment. Thus, in the recession years—1975–1976, 1982–1983, and 1991–1992— the actual deficit was larger than the high-employment deficit. Only during the boom years of the Vietnam War was the actual deficit smaller. For the entire period shown here, the average deficits were approximately equal: 2.46 percent of GDP for the actual deficit and 2.36 percent for the high-employment deficit. But the actual deficit was much more variable.

HIGH-EMPLOYMENT DEFICITS AS PERCENTAGE OF POTENTIAL GDP AND ACTUAL DEFICITS AS PERCENTAGE OF ACTUAL GDP, 1962–1998

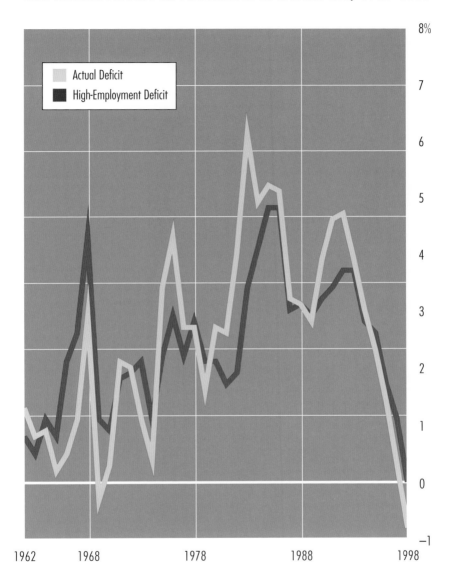

Different plausible definitions yield very different calculations of the size of the federal deficit or surplus.

There are two main reasons for measuring the aggregate relation between revenues and expenditure, that is, the deficit and the surplus. One is a disciplinary reason, to keep track of how extensively, if at all, the government is giving benefits to people, through expenditures, without assessing the costs, through taxes. This concern may be operative even when there is a surplus, because whether an increase of expenditures relative to revenues is reducing the surplus is also a significant fact for budget discipline. The other reason for measuring the net budget position is to see how much, if at all, the government is subtracting from or adding to total national savings by running a deficit or surplus, and so subtracting from or adding to total investment.

Although measurements of the deficit or the surplus are useful for these purposes, no single measure or combination of measures is completely satisfactory. The government can provide benefits that do not appear in any measure of contemporary expenditures, for example, by implementing legislation that gives benefits to be paid for in the future or by mandating states, localities, and private parties to provide benefits to others, or by giving them tax incentives for the same purpose. The government also affects investment by promising future benefits that influence private saving and by the character of its taxes.

The chart shows estimates of the surplus for fiscal 1998 on five plausible definitions:

  A. The conventional "cash-consolidated" definition: the relation between all cash receipts and all cash expenditures.
  B. The government's gross savings (positive or negative), which are, with minor exceptions, definition A plus federal investment. Making allowance for state and local government surpluses, this definition fits into the equation that the surplus plus private savings plus the capital inflow from abroad equals gross domestic investment.
  C. The government balance on current account, which is the foregoing less depreciation of government assets.
  D. The change in a comprehensive measure of the net liabilities of the federal government, including the Federal Reserve system, taking account of the value of capital assets such as infrastructure and gold, all adjusted for inflation, but not counting implicit obligations such as the accrued obligations of the Social Security system.
  E. The amount by which the surplus of type A exceeds the deficit that would keep the ratio of federal debt to GDP constant.

FEDERAL BUDGET SURPLUS, BY VARIOUS DEFINITIONS, FISCAL 1998

BILLIONS OF DOLLARS

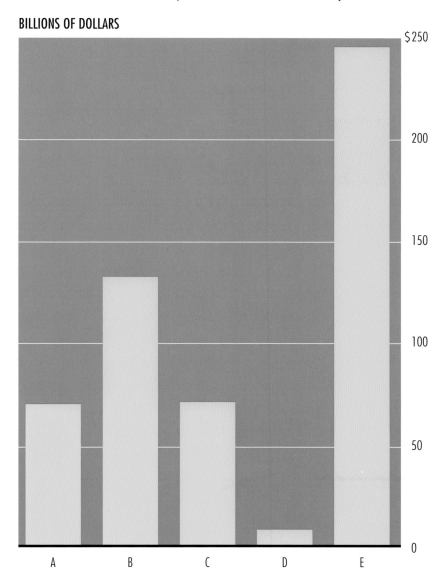

PART FOURTEEN

Health

National health expenditures were $1.1 trillion in 1997, or 13.5 percent of GDP.

According to the Health Care Financing Administration (HCFA), 88.7 percent of national health expenditures covered personal health care in 1997 (top chart). The remainder represented the net cost of private health insurance (premiums less benefits) and of the administrative expense of government programs such as Medicare and Medicaid (4.6 percent); government public health activities (3.5 percent); and research and hospital construction (3.2 percent). Personal health care means spending for hospital services, doctors and dentists, drugs and medicines, nursing homes, home health care, wheelchairs, eyeglasses, and so forth. The other categories of expenditures—private insurance, research, hospital construction, and public health programs—are arbitrary, since persons are the ultimate beneficiaries of all health expenditures.

Private insurance costs in 1997 were $35 billion. This represents the difference between insurance premiums of $348 billion and benefits of $313 billion, which represent 32 percent and 29 percent of national health expenditures. The premiums are paid by employers and employees in employer-sponsored plans as well as by individuals for their own policies. Private insurance embraces not only conventional health insurance but also Blue Cross–Blue Shield, health maintenance organizations, and arrangements such as preferred provider organizations.

In 1965, when Medicare and Medicaid were enacted, national health expenditures were only 5.7 percent of GDP, and personal health care only 5.0 percent. The increased shares of GDP can be attributed to new government programs, the rise of incomes generally, and the spread of private health insurance. In 1965, the net cost of private insurance and the administrative cost of running government programs were somewhat lower (4.4 percent), the public health share was much lower (1.4 percent), and research and hospital construction were much higher (7.9 percent).

The bottom chart shows breakdowns of expenditures in 1965 and 1997 as estimated by HCFA. In 1997, the largest share of the consumer health dollar went to hospitals, followed by physicians' services. The shares for other professional services and for drugs and medicines were about equal. Changes in percentage shares from 1965 to 1997, which reflect changes in both prices and physical volume, are striking for drugs and medicines, whose share fell drastically, and for nursing home care, whose share rose considerably. Both the hospital share and the share taken by doctors declined.

NATIONAL HEALTH EXPENDITURES, BY TYPE OF EXPENDITURE, 1997

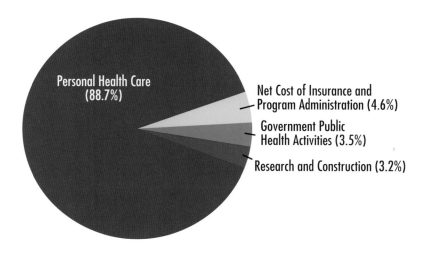

Personal Health Care (88.7%)

Net Cost of Insurance and Program Administration (4.6%)

Government Public Health Activities (3.5%)

Research and Construction (3.2%)

DISTRIBUTION OF PERSONAL HEALTH EXPENDITURES, BY TYPE, 1965 AND 1997

PERCENT

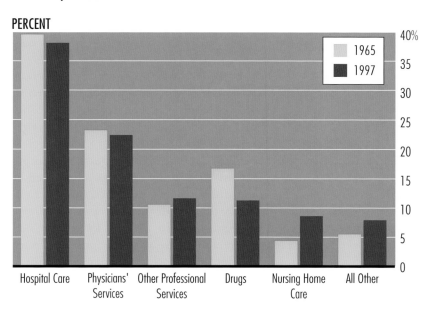

Increases in the prices and output of the health services industry have slowed in recent years, but the data leave many questions unanswered.

When consumers make expenditures for medical care, they purchase the output of several industries. Most important is the health services industry, including hospitals (excluding government hospitals), private doctors and dentists, medical labs, and the like. Consumer expenditures for medical care also pay for the output of the pharmaceutical industry (drugs and medicines); the food industry (food eaten in hospitals and nursing homes); the eyeglass industry; and many others.

From 1947 to 1977, the output of the health services industry grew much faster than average, but that experience has not been repeated. From 1977 to 1993 (top chart), the physical volume of the output of health services grew at an annual rate of only 2.2 percent, as compared with a rate of 2.7 percent for all private industries. The difference in price change over this same period was striking: more than 8 percent per year for health services, compared with 4.8 percent for all domestic private industries.

Despite the slow growth in output from 1977 to 1993, employment in the health services industry grew at double the all–private industry rate. This employment growth implies a deterioration in productivity and rising labor costs per unit of output.

From 1993 to 1997, slower rates of inflation showed up for the private sector as a whole, as well as for the health services industry. However, an acceleration in output growth for the private industry sector was not matched in health services. Indeed, output growth in the health services industry slowed down (see bottom chart).

Serious questions can be raised about measured changes in the output of health services. In simplest terms, the output measures are derived by dividing expenditures in current dollars by price indexes, but the price indexes have an upward bias. They do not adequately capture improvements in quality resulting from advances in medical knowledge and technological change. A fundamental problem is that the prices collected typically focus on intermediate inputs, such as the cost of an office visit to a doctor or the cost of a night in a hospital. We really want to know about final outcomes, that is, the health and well-being of the patient. Research addressing this sort of problem is going on, but it is still at an early stage. Measurement problems of price indexes in the health field are discussed further in part fifteen.

ANNUAL RATE OF CHANGE IN OUTPUT, PRICES, AND EMPLOYMENT IN THE HEALTH SERVICES INDUSTRY AND ALL PRIVATE INDUSTRY, 1977–1993

PERCENT

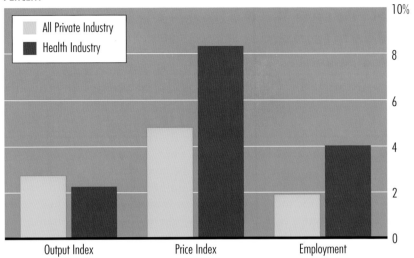

ANNUAL RATE OF CHANGE IN OUTPUT, PRICES, AND EMPLOYMENT IN THE HEALTH SERVICES INDUSTRY AND ALL PRIVATE INDUSTRY, 1993–1997

PERCENT

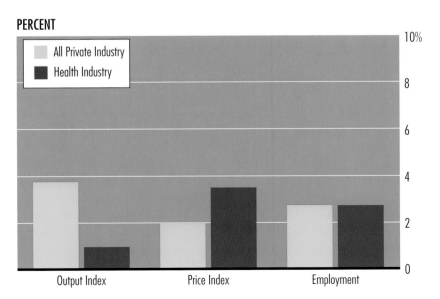

Since the 1960s, the out-of-pocket share of expenditures for health care has declined, while the share of third-party payments has increased.

In 1965, when Medicare and Medicaid were enacted, individuals made out-of-pocket payments for 51 percent of their health care expenditures. Private health insurance accounted for about one-fourth of the total and government for about the same share. At that time, the government share meant mainly the federal Veterans Administration hospitals and state and local hospitals and clinics.

Since then, as the chart shows, striking changes have occurred. Probably the most important economically is the sharp decline in the importance of out-of-pocket payments, which fell to 21.7 percent of the personal health care total in 1997, and the complementary rise in third-party payments. Combined, Medicare and Medicaid now finance more than one-third of the total, and private insurance accounts for just under one-third. In recent years, the employer share of private insurance has decreased, as the growth of employer-provided health benefits has slowed considerably. The long-standing government programs now account for only 12 percent, but government as a whole finances 47 percent of total expenditures, not counting taxes forgone.

Analysts point to the decline in out-of-pocket payments as the most important reason for the rapid escalation in health care costs in the last one-third of the twentieth century and for the distortions brought on by a partially regulated health care system. Taxpayers at all levels pay for Medicaid, whose benefits go to low-income persons. Medicaid payments to hospitals and doctors reimburse much less than the costs incurred. To a lesser extent, this is true also of Medicare, which covers older and disabled people regardless of income and is paid for by payroll taxes on employers and employees, by premiums, and by general revenues. These Medicare and Medicaid services are provided by the health care industry, which makes up for inadequate government payments by shifting costs to all other patients, especially to those without any kind of health insurance.

What is not known about the U.S. health care system, with its high costs and many distortions, is how the health of the population has been affected. We do not know whether the same health services could have been obtained at lower cost or whether the high costs that seem so common have, in fact, brought about better results that are not now obvious on some comprehensive basis.

PERCENTAGE DISTRIBUTION OF PERSONAL HEALTH EXPENDITURES, BY SOURCE OF FINANCING, 1960–1997

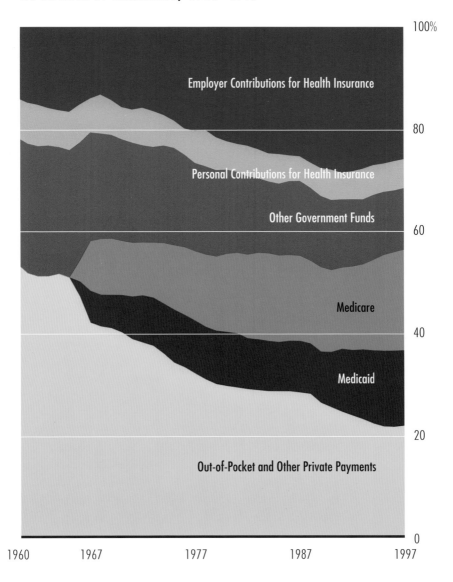

Employer Contributions for Health Insurance

Personal Contributions for Health Insurance

Other Government Funds

Medicare

Medicaid

Out-of-Pocket and Other Private Payments

100%

80

60

40

20

0

1960   1967   1977   1987   1997

Most persons who have health insurance provided by employers enjoy a large subsidy.

A large part of the population covered by health insurance is being subsidized by the government. The benefits come at the expense of those not covered by insurance or of those who buy their own. Employees have always had the option of taking part of their compensation in the form of nontaxable fringe benefits rather than taxable wages or salaries. With some exceptions, people who buy their own insurance cannot deduct any medical expenses from taxable income. In addition, self-employed persons have been able to deduct part of their insurance premiums since 1987. The Joint Committee on Taxation has estimated a tax loss of $58 billion for fiscal year 1999 because of the exclusion of employer contributions for health care, health insurance premiums, and long-term care insurance premiums.

In 1997, about three of every four persons were covered by insurance. Most insurance is provided by a person's employer or by the employers of other family members.

The Congressional Budget Office has estimated for the year 1992—the last time such a study was done—the average tax subsidy of employment-based health insurance to families by size of family income. The average subsidy was estimated to be $1,130, which was 26 percent of the average premium. That proportion rose from 11 percent for families with income below $10,000 to 33 percent for families with incomes of $200,000 or more. The charts illustrate three other points.

- As a percentage of after-tax income for families with employment-based health insurance, the subsidy varied from 2 to 3.5 percent over a broad range of incomes.
- As a percentage of after-tax income for all families—those with and those without employer-based insurance—the percentage rose as income rose, reaching about 2.3 percent at $20,000 and staying at about that level, except for families with incomes above $100,000.
- The after-tax premium was 7 percent of after-tax income for all families. It was 9–10 percent for families with after-tax income of $20,000–50,000.

TAX SUBSIDY AS PERCENTAGE OF AFTER-TAX INCOME, BY INCOME CLASS, 1992

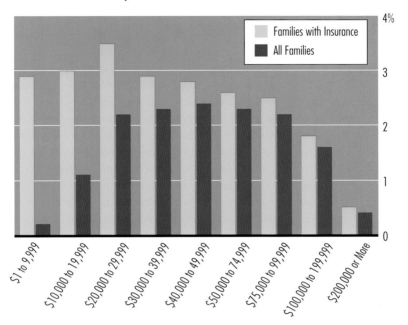

PREMIUM AS PERCENTAGE OF INCOME, BY INCOME CLASS, 1992

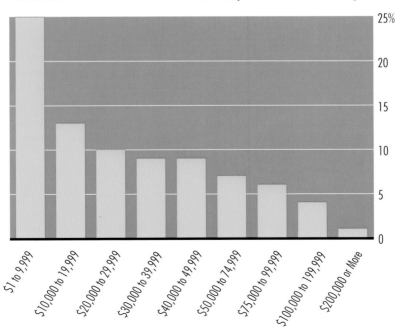

In 1997, 16 percent of the population was not covered by health insurance.

The lack of any kind of health insurance was one of the main reasons that health care became a major political issue in 1993 and 1994. The rise in the proportion of the population without health insurance that was evident earlier in the 1990s has continued, despite the robust economy since that time (see top chart).

The category of those without insurance embraces working people with incomes too high to qualify for Medicaid but too low to buy insurance. The sharp rise in health care costs noted on page 242 was accompanied by a rapid escalation in the costs of health insurance, a development that explains some of the rise illustrated in the top chart. The noninsured category also includes those, especially young adults, who could buy insurance but prefer not to, because they consider the risk of a costly illness too low. Census data indicate that, in 1997, the lack of insurance among persons aged eighteen to twenty-four was almost double the rate for all age groups.

Insurance coverage data based on Census Bureau surveys show an inverse relationship between the level of household income and the lack of health insurance (see bottom chart). The differences in coverage by income class are probably smaller than shown in the chart. For example, the Census Bureau calls attention to the fact that its estimates of Medicare and Medicaid coverage are lower than the coverage statistics of the Health Care Financing Administration. The census estimates are based on a sample survey; the survey's focus was not health insurance coverage, whereas the HCFA figures purport to be a complete count of program participants. The Census Bureau notes that many people do not know if they or their children have health insurance; this condition is more likely to be found among low-income groups.

Despite the fact that much is not known about the uninsured, there can be little doubt that the absence of health insurance for many millions of persons is a continuing problem for the society.

PERCENT OF POPULATION NOT COVERED BY HEALTH INSURANCE, 1987–1997

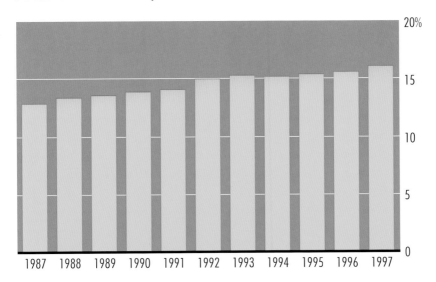

LACK OF HEALTH INSURANCE COVERAGE, BY HOUSEHOLD INCOME, 1997

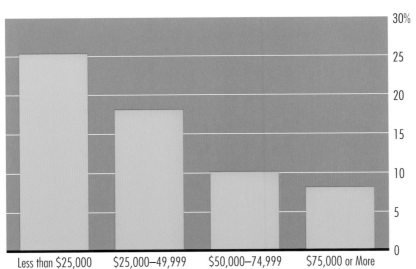

PART FIFTEEN

Price Indexes and the Quality of Life

Conventional measures of economic progress— such as real GDP or consumption per capita—leave much to be desired, despite their usefulness.

Some measurement problems involving GDP remain inherently difficult; of these, measuring price change is the hardest. For all the care the price indexes receive from the Bureau of Labor Statistics, many problems persist. In December 1996, an advisory commission headed by Michael Boskin reported to a Senate committee that the consumer price index was subject to an upward bias of about 1 percentage point (1.1) a year. The commission noted three main types of bias, which are partly overlapping: (1) those due to the treatment of quality change and new products; (2) those due to "substitution bias" (explained on page 254); and (3) those due to a failure to keep up with new types of outlets. The BLS took issue with many specific criticisms, but it did change some of its procedures—a reflection of both its own work in progress and a response to the commission's criticisms. We believe that the CPI is biased upward, but we do not know by how much.

The chart gives a breakdown of the sources of upward bias as estimated by the Boskin commission. The most important bias noted involves the treatment of quality change and the related problem of the treatment of new products or innovations. The BLS approach to measuring price change is the *market basket* approach, that is, establishing a set of goods and services based on consumer buying patterns and measuring their prices every month or periodically. At the heart of this approach is *specification pricing*. To measure a price change from month 1 to month 2, BLS tries to ensure that the item being priced in month 2 is the same item priced in month 1. For each item, the bureau establishes specifications that describe the item's characteristics as well as the type of retail store selling the item. Goods and services offered for sale are not static, however; frequent model changes are common. Suppliers can vary quality and prices at the same time or may hold prices constant and vary quality. Keeping track of these price-mixed-with-quality changes can be difficult.

The outlet bias comes from a failure to keep up with changing market structure. BLS has treated a given item sold in a chain store differently from the identical item sold by a small independent, because the two types of stores offer different services. The effect of the trend toward chains with their lower prices is partly missed.

SOURCES OF BIAS IN THE CONSUMER PRICE INDEX
AS ESTIMATED BY THE BOSKIN COMMISSION, DECEMBER 1996

PERCENTAGE POINTS PER YEAR

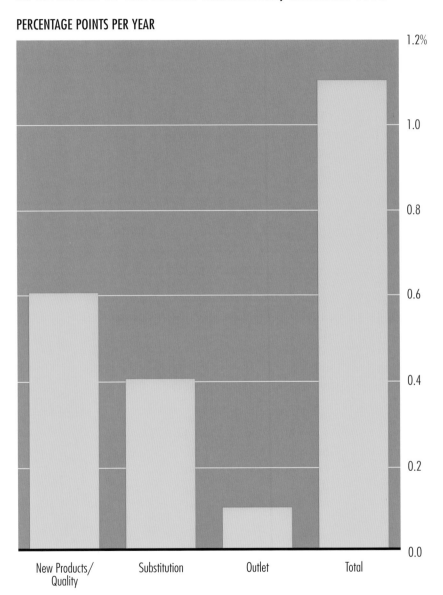

Note: Numbers denote estimated overstatement of the price rise.

Price indexes with fixed base-period weights have an upward bias.

A price index combines, or aggregates, prices of various items into a single statistic. There are many different ways of combining—that is, different formulas—but there is no perfect way. Until the end of 1998, the consumer price index always reflected the use of fixed base-period weights. Weights are primarily based on surveys of consumer expenditures and have been changed periodically so that the index may reflect a more up-to-date market basket of goods and services. The most important updating has typically been carried out about every ten years; that updating is supplemented with information from ongoing surveys.

A price index reflecting base-period weights suffers from what economists call *substitution bias*. Substitution bias arises because, as relative prices change, consumers shift their purchases away from items with prices that have risen the most toward items with prices that have risen least or may have fallen.

In this regard, a price index with a superior formula for combining price changes is the *geometric mean index*, which suffers much less from this kind of substitution bias and is a good approximation of how consumers behave. In 1998, to see how much of a difference an alternative index would make, the BLS published a comparison of two indexes that differed only to the extent that they were calculated with different formulas. From December 1990 to December 1997, the geometric mean index rose at an average annual rate of 2.3 percent, whereas the comparable CPI rose at a rate of 2.6 percent (see chart).

In January 1999, the BLS changed some of its price index formulas to reflect the use of the geometric mean. The bureau has noted that the new type of aggregation—combining different price changes into a single figure—is being used extensively at the most detailed level. For example, the formula is used to combine price changes of one variety of apple with those of another variety to make up a price category called *apples*. However, the CPI still has substitution biases at broader levels. For example, price changes of apples are not being combined with those of oranges to constitute, say, *fresh fruit*. Substitution biases due to differential price movements in apples as compared with oranges remain in the index. This is true also of substitution among entire important categories of expenditure, for example, clothing compared with food.

EFFECTS OF NEW FORMULA ON THE CALCULATION OF THE CONSUMER PRICE INDEX, DECEMBER 1990–DECEMBER 1997

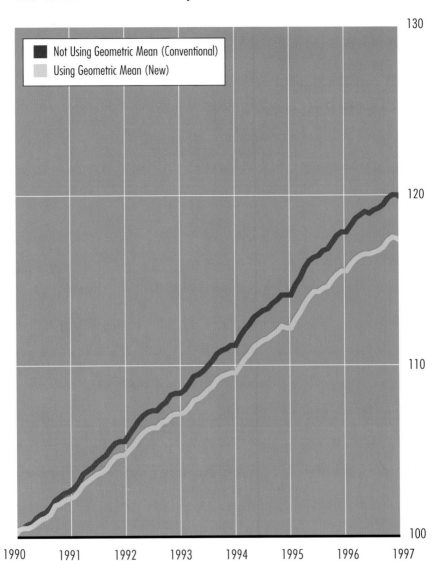

Not Using Geometric Mean (Conventional)
Using Geometric Mean (New)

In price measurement, the treatment of innovations or new products is perhaps the most difficult aspect of handling quality change.

New products and services are constantly appearing. Knowing how to treat them in a price index has perplexed economists and statisticians. The problem has many facets. For example, the characteristics of some new products are unique so that price comparisons of today, with the new product, and yesterday, with the old product, are impossible. At the initial date, when the new product appears in the price index, there is a break with the past. Consequently, the welfare gain represented by the innovation is omitted. For some products, price comparisons are possible in principle, but they are not made in a market basket index. Television drastically reduced the price of entertainment, but, in the consumer price index, the price of services of a television set has not been compared with the price of a ticket to the movies or a baseball game.

The time an innovation is introduced into a price index presents still another problem. The BLS once waited until a new product was "seasoned," that is, was well established in the market, before its prices became a part of an official index. The official index would miss all or much of the big price drop that typically characterizes a new product early in its life. Indeed, that price decline is an important reason the product will experience rapid growth. Of course, the weight of a new product is typically small early in its market life, but the price decline is often so large that omitting this very early phase gives an upward bias to a price index. At present the BLS is handling this issue in a much better fashion than formerly.

The chart illustrates the chain price index being used by the Bureau of Economic Analysis of the Commerce Department for computers and equipment. This represents a vast improvement over an earlier procedure. Until the mid-1980s, lacking price indexes from the Labor Department and not knowing how to measure computer prices, the Commerce Department assumed no change in the nominal price of computers.

PRICE INDEX FOR COMPUTERS, 1960–1998

INDEX: 1992=100, LOGARITHMIC SCALE

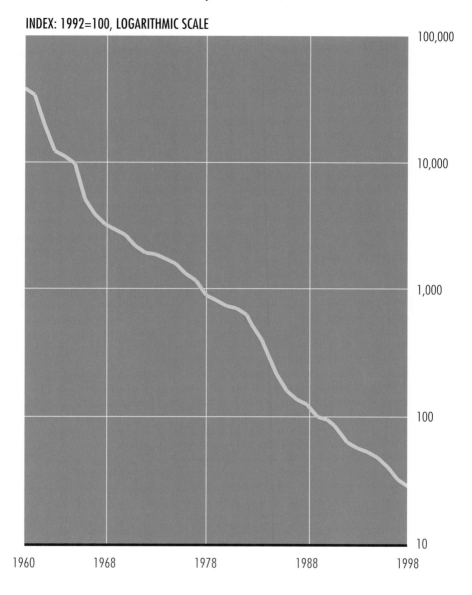

Aside from the difficulties of price measurement, GDP is not a measure of welfare.

Our well-being and how much our lives have improved over the years depend on much more than flows of goods and services that pass through markets. Hours spent off the job in housework and raising children are also important. Our well-being depends on how much leisure we have, on the social and political conditions under which we do our paid and unpaid work and spend our leisure hours, on our health as well as on our physical environment, and on the public capital and the private capital that we have in the form of housing and consumer durables. The last point is illustrated in the top chart, which shows the ownership of various consumer durables in 1997. All households have refrigerators, practically all have gas or electric ranges, and 98 percent own color TVs. Thirty-five percent of all households in the United States had a personal computer in 1997.

These aspects of everyday living are so common today that they are taken for granted, but that was not so early in the twentieth century. Some examples of how things have changed are shown in the bottom chart, which illustrates the prevalence of electricity, complete plumbing facilities, and telephones since 1900. Even as recently as 1940, only 55 percent of households had complete plumbing facilities, and in 1960, one of five households lacked a telephone. Although these figures point to genuine progress, a fundamental problem remains: statistics alone cannot capture the convenience of electric lighting, of private indoor toilet facilities, and of a telephone in the home.

A generation ago, when economists began to show greater interest in how to measure changes in well-being—for worse as well as for better—it was fashionable to discuss traffic congestion, the increase in commuting time, and environmental problems. Today, social problems have come to the fore. We have statistics on crime and illegitimacy, but it is not enough to point to the long-run increase in crime and illegitimate births. The problem, which is probably unsolvable, is to put all these statistics together in a unified framework embracing what is already included in measured real per capita income or consumption.

PERCENTAGE OF HOUSEHOLDS OWNING VARIOUS DURABLE GOODS, 1997

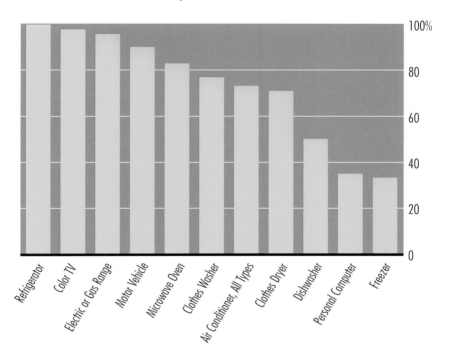

PERCENTAGE OF U.S. HOMES WITH VARIOUS AMENITIES, 1900–1996

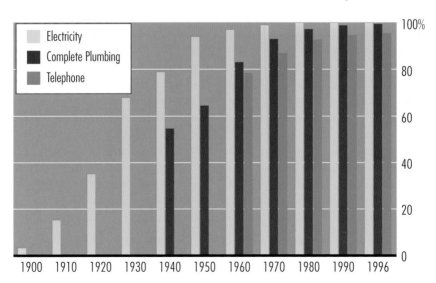

Environmental issues highlight the difficulties economists have in assessing how welfare has been affected.

From 1972 to 1993, real expenditures by consumers, business, and government for pollution abatement and control increased by almost 120 percent. The relative rise in business expenditures for pollution control was almost as large (see top chart). Over the same period, business GDP rose about 80 percent.

Expenditures for pollution control increase costs and become part of measured GDP, but whether they should be included is a matter of debate. They are made to restore the natural environment to a previously superior condition and to prevent future pollution. Their inclusion exaggerates the growth of productivity and real income. According to Edward Denison, however, any correction for the overstatement in productivity growth should be limited to those expenditures made by business, not by what consumers and governments spend. Focusing on *measured* GDP, Denison argued that if consumers did not make expenditures for emission abatement devices on their automobiles, they would probably make expenditures of comparable size on other things. The same is true of such expenditures by government. New pollution regulations imposed on business, however, require businesses to incur costs that they would not otherwise have incurred. The regulations give us a cleaner and healthier environment than would be found without them, but the resources used could ultimately have been devoted to other consumption.

The productivity data used in this book do not make allowance for the fact that business pollution expenditures rose more than business GDP. If they did, the growth in productivity from 1972 to 1993 would have to be reduced, but only slightly, because these expenditures were only a little more than 1 percent of the business product.

What can be said about the benefits? Although cleaner air and water are genuine benefits, they are not now part of measured GDP, nor are the health benefits that come from a cleaner environment. The determination and calculation of these benefits pose a formidable problem. Thus, although many common air pollutants have decreased since 1970 in the face of rising economic activity and automobile use (see bottom chart), our current national accounts do not show the benefits. The short-lived satellite accounts discussed elsewhere were a step in the right direction.

POLLUTION ABATEMENT EXPENDITURES BY SECTOR, 1972–1993

BILLIONS OF CHAINED 1992 DOLLARS

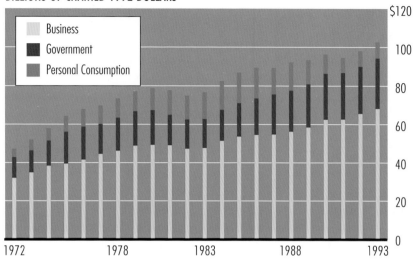

Legend:
- Business
- Government
- Personal Consumption

1972   1978   1983   1988   1993

NATIONAL AIR POLLUTANT EMISSIONS, BY POLLUTANT, 1940–1997

1970 QUANTITIES=100

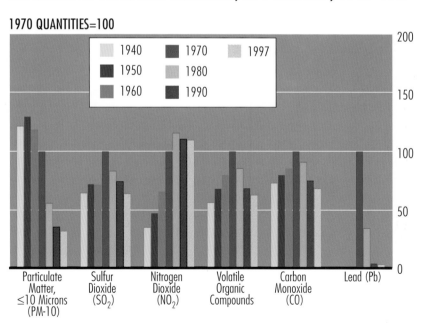

Legend:
- 1940
- 1950
- 1960
- 1970
- 1980
- 1990
- 1997

Particulate Matter, ≤10 Microns (PM-10) · Sulfur Dioxide (SO₂) · Nitrogen Dioxide (NO₂) · Volatile Organic Compounds · Carbon Monoxide (CO) · Lead (Pb)

Attempts to construct indexes of economic welfare have not gained widespread acceptance.

Economists have tried to go beyond the market-based national income and product accounts to obtain a closer approximation of welfare. That involves "pushing out the boundaries" of what is already measured. The most common extensions make imputations for the services of certain kinds of fixed capital not now included. In this country, that category would mean the services of consumer capital, since the services of government capital are now part of the accounts. The extensions would also cover the value of housework performed by the housewife, and in some instances, the value of leisure "consumed" by individuals.

More recently, some researchers have broadened the definition of capital formation to embrace formal education, child-rearing, and activities that maintain a family's health. Valuation problems are difficult where no market exists. Should housework, for example, be valued at the cost of hiring a housekeeper or at the hourly wage the (working) housewife earns on her job? Comparisons over time require inflation adjustments, but whether the deflator should be the wage rate or the CPI is not clear.

Several economists have undertaken these efforts. Because they cover more activities, their totals have been greater than the official GNP or GDP totals. The chart illustrates estimates of Robert Eisner in his total-incomes system of accounts (TISA) and an earlier version of the official U.S. constant-dollar GNP from 1946 to 1981. Summarizing the results of the expanded measures—his own as well as others—Professor Eisner noted that the alternatives did not grow as fast from the early postwar period to the early 1980s, but that differences were not major. The alternatives, like the official figures, show a slowdown in real growth starting in the mid-1970s.

Another line of research has involved the development of *social indicators* pertaining to health, crime, the environment, and many other aspects of welfare. In some fashion, these would be combined with conventional measures of real income or consumption per capita. That task is much harder, because social indicators go far more beyond the market than the extended accounts discussed above. Aside from that, if individual preferences vary, how are they to be combined? Earlier research on social indicators was criticized because it lacked a good theoretical framework. Although social problems have become more important than before, we are still a long way from having a measure that would be widely accepted.

OFFICIAL GNP MEASURE AND TOTAL INCOMES SYSTEM OF ACCOUNTS MEASURE OF REAL OUTPUT, 1946–1981

BILLIONS OF CONSTANT DOLLARS, LOGARITHMIC SCALE

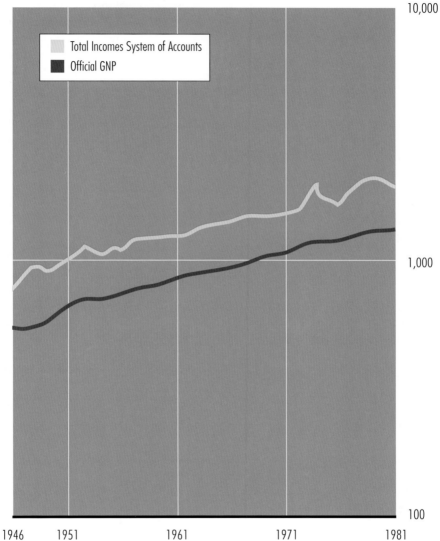

PART SIXTEEN

The United States in the World Economy

Since the 1960s, U.S. international economic transactions have increased greatly as a percentage of GDP.

The chart shows total payments and receipts on current account—that is, it excludes capital transactions such as investment flows in or out of the country. The payments included are for the purchase of goods and services, investment income, and unilateral transfers, such as private remittances and foreign aid. The largest item on both sides is the export or import of merchandise, although the international flow of services has become increasingly important.

The increase in foreign transactions relative to GDP resulted in part from reductions of tariffs and other governmental barriers to international trade and from reductions in the costs of transportation and communication. With lower obstacles to trade in goods and services, countries could concentrate on producing the things at which they were relatively efficient, and they and their customers could gain the benefits of specialization and large-scale production. The increase in international economic transactions has also resulted from large increases in real incomes, especially among the industrial countries but also, more and more, among the newly emerging economies. As incomes have risen, people have become more willing and able to pay for variety in their consumption, including travel. And they have often found variety in foreign products and places.

The greater access of Americans to foreign goods and services, and their increased purchase of them, have improved their standard of living—partly because of the foreign products consumed directly and partly because of the importation of capital goods that has increased productivity. At the same time, the enlarged foreign markets have enabled American businesses and their employees to concentrate on the kinds of production they do best and so to increase their real incomes. Some American businesses and their employees have suffered from the increase of foreign competition, just as some businesses and workers have suffered as a result of increased competition from other American businesses and workers. But there is no doubt that the increase in foreign transactions has been a substantial net benefit to Americans.

FOREIGN PAYMENTS AND RECEIPTS AS PERCENTAGE OF GDP, 1929–1998

EXCLUDING CAPITAL FLOWS

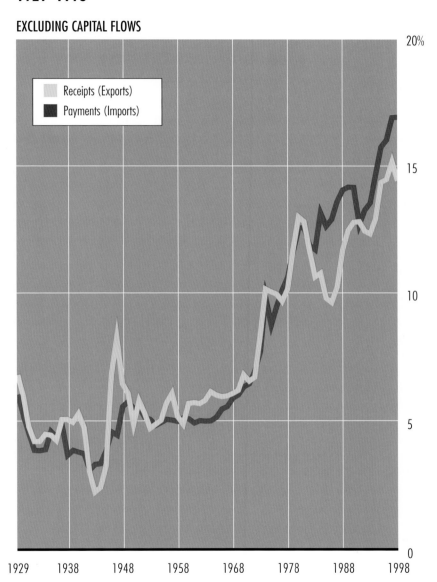

Receipts (Exports)
Payments (Imports)

20%

15

10

5

0

1929   1938   1948   1958   1968   1978   1988   1998

Since the early 1980s, U.S. payments abroad, excluding capital transactions, have exceeded U.S. receipts from the rest of the world—a highly unusual situation for the United States in the twentieth century.

In the early days of American history, when the rest of the world was investing heavily in the development of the American economy, U.S. payments to the rest of the world—primarily for the import of goods—typically exceeded U.S. receipts from the rest of the world—primarily for the export of goods. But, since 1870, that has been rare. As the chart shows, there was a brief exception during World War II when U.S. receipts from the rest of the world fell sharply below payments. That happened because most U.S. exports were not sold but were provided by the U.S. government to the Allies under Lend-Lease or otherwise. Thus, the excess of payments that began in the 1980s, and especially the magnitude it reached after 1992, came as a surprise.

The large increase in U.S. expenditures for imports of petroleum products after 1973, when the oil price had its first sharp rise, was an element in the shift from an excess of receipts to an excess of payments. But even when the cost of imports of petroleum products is excluded, the United States has had an excess of payments since 1983, except for 1991. In 1998, the excess of payments was 17 percent of receipts—13 percent if the costs of oil imports are excluded.

It is important to note that the excess of U.S. payments shown here excludes the receipts from foreign investment in the United States. The relation between the receipts from foreign investment and the net payments on other transactions is discussed on pages 274 and 278.

EXCESS OF FOREIGN RECEIPTS OVER PAYMENTS AS PERCENTAGE OF TOTAL FOREIGN RECEIPTS, 1929–1998

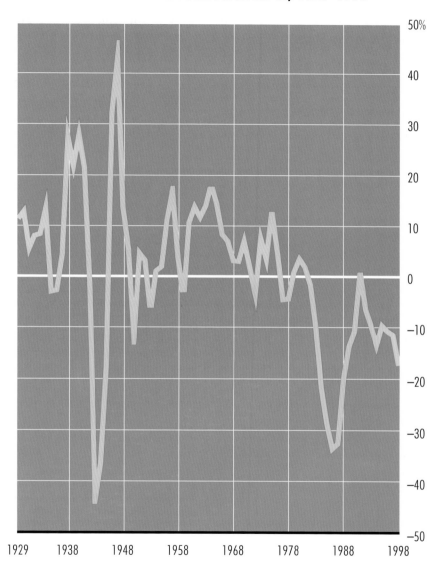

Since 1981, as both imports and exports have increased, the geographical composition of foreign trade has changed greatly.

The big change has been the increase in the proportion of our trade, both imports and exports, with Asian nations other than Japan. U.S. exports to that part of the world increased from 12 to 20 percent of our total exports, while imports from that area increased from 12 to 24 percent. The increase reflected the rapid economic growth of those countries, which included China and South Korea, making them more important as both suppliers and customers of the United States.

In the other direction, the proportion of our trade with the oil-producing countries declined. The value of exports to them fell from 9 percent of our total exports to 3 percent, and the value of imports, almost all oil and oil products, fell from 19 percent to 5.2 percent. The volume of oil imports, measured in barrels, increased by 58 percent, while the price of oil per barrel fell by 45 percent. The dollar value of our imports from the member-countries of the Organization of Petroleum Exporting Countries (OPEC) fell by 11 percent, while the value of our total imports tripled.

The net of these changes in the distribution of exports and imports was a big shift in the location of our trade deficit. In 1981, when our deficit with the OPEC countries exceeded our total deficit, we had a surplus with the rest of the world as a whole, mainly with Western Europe. By 1986, our deficit with the OPEC countries had shrunk to 13 percent of our total deficit. The deficit with the Asian countries other than Japan had risen from 14 percent to 37 percent.

None of these figures show the effects of the major slowdowns in some Asian countries that occurred in 1998. That crisis will almost certainly reduce the share of those countries in our trade, at least in our exports. The duration of this effect is uncertain.

An excess of total international payments over receipts does not signal a problem. This is even more true for an excess of payments to a particular country. If not invested in the United States, the dollars that a country—say, China—earns in transactions with the United States will be paid to another country, which will use them either to buy goods and services here or to invest here.

EXPORTS OF GOODS BY DESTINATION, 1981 AND 1997

BILLIONS OF CHAINED 1992 DOLLARS

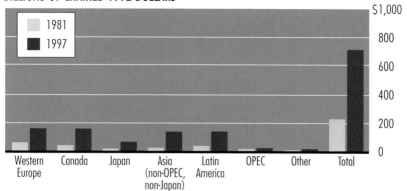

IMPORTS OF GOODS BY SOURCE, 1981 AND 1997

BILLIONS OF CHAINED 1992 DOLLARS

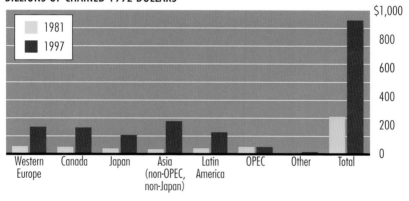

EXCESS OF IMPORTS OVER EXPORTS OF GOODS, 1981 AND 1997

BILLIONS OF CHAINED 1992 DOLLARS

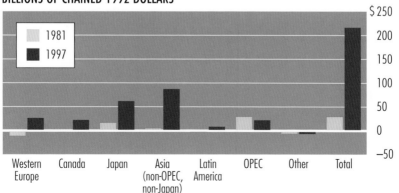

More than one-third of U.S. foreign trade is between companies affiliated here and abroad.

It is a sign of the high degree of internationalization of economic business that, in 1995, 32 percent of all U.S. exports went to foreign companies affiliated with U.S. companies and 38 percent of U.S. imports came from foreign companies affiliated with U.S companies. Sales from parent companies to their foreign affiliates were the main factor in these interfirm transactions in both directions. Twenty-three percent of our exports went to foreign affiliates of U.S. parent companies, and 9 percent of exports from the United States went to foreign parents of affiliates in the United States. On the import side, 23 percent came from foreign parents of U.S. affiliates, and 15 percent came from foreign affiliates of U.S. parents.

FOREIGN TRADE WITH AFFILIATES, 1995

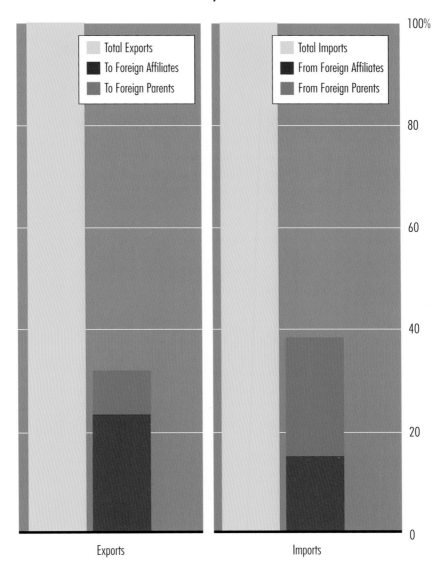

Exports legend:
- Total Exports
- To Foreign Affiliates
- To Foreign Parents

Imports legend:
- Total Imports
- From Foreign Affiliates
- From Foreign Parents

Exports

Imports

Net American payments to foreigners for imports equal net investment by foreigners in the United States.

When Americans buy more from the rest of the world than they sell abroad and when the U.S. government or private Americans make payments to foreigners, the foreigners acquire dollars. They can keep the dollars in American banks, or they can invest them in other kinds of assets in this country, such as government securities, American stocks or bonds, American real estate, or American businesses. An individual foreigner can exchange dollars for some other kind of asset that is not an investment in the United States. In that case, another foreigner is then holding the dollars. If the dollars are not used to buy goods and services from the United States or to make gifts to Americans, the rest of the world can do nothing with them except to invest them here.

The same process works in reverse if the United States is a net earner of foreign currency. The Americans can do nothing with that currency but invest it abroad. If all transactions are accounted for, there can be no deficit in the balance of payments.

In 1980, the foreign receipts of Americans from exports of goods and services and from earnings on foreign investment exceeded American payments to foreigners by $13 billion. That amount was invested by Americans abroad. In 1998, Americans paid $1,441 billion to foreigners for purchases of goods and services, for the earnings from investments here, and for transfers, mainly by the U.S. government. Foreigners paid $1,228 billion to Americans for the purchase of goods and services and for the earnings of American investors abroad. The difference—the excess $213 billion received by foreigners—was invested in the United States.

The chart at the bottom of the facing page shows the great variation in the size of this foreign investment, called the *capital inflow*, during the 1980s and 1990s. The reasons for these variations are discussed on the following pages.

BALANCE OF PAYMENTS, 1980 AND 1998

BILLIONS OF DOLLARS

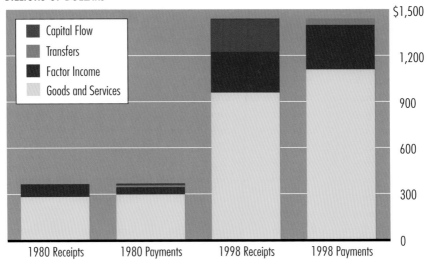

Legend:
- Capital Flow
- Transfers
- Factor Income
- Goods and Services

y-axis: $1,500 / 1,200 / 900 / 600 / 300 / 0

x-axis: 1980 Receipts | 1980 Payments | 1998 Receipts | 1998 Payments

CAPITAL INFLOW TO THE UNITED STATES, 1946–1998

BILLIONS OF DOLLARS

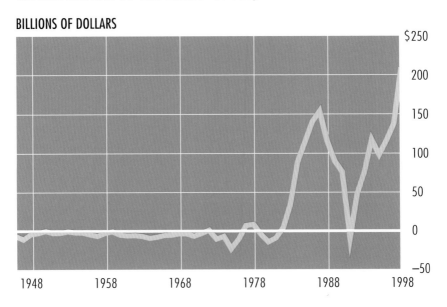

y-axis: $250 / 200 / 150 / 100 / 50 / 0 / −50

x-axis: 1948 | 1958 | 1968 | 1978 | 1988 | 1998

The dollar exchange rate rose sharply in the early 1980s but then fell back to about the level of the 1970s.

The dollar exchange rate is the price of a dollar in a specified foreign currency. Thus, in 1997, on the average, the yen exchange rate was 121.06; that is, the price of a dollar was 121.06 yen.

Exchange rates, like other prices, are determined in markets by the supply and demand for the things that are to be exchanged. When the quantity of dollars that people want to sell at the existing exchange rate exceeds the quantity that people want to buy, the exchange rate of the dollar falls.

The exchange rate is an important factor in determining the competitiveness of the products of different countries. The higher the dollar is, the more expensive U.S. products are for foreigners and the less of them they will buy, and the cheaper foreign products are for Americans, the more of them Americans will buy.

Between 1978 and 1985, the dollar, relative to the yen, rose by 13.3 percent, from 210 yen to the dollar to 238, as shown in the top chart. (The yen is used as an illustration only, not because it has unique qualities.) That movement increased the competitiveness of Japanese products relative to U.S. products. In the same period, the U.S. price level (consumer price index) rose by 65 percent, whereas the Japanese price level rose by 28 percent. That is a crude measure of what happened to the relative costs of U.S. and Japanese products in their home markets. When the two factors—the exchange rate and the price levels—are combined, the amount of Japanese product that could be obtained for a dollar relative to the U.S. product rose by 46 percent. That is a measure of the change in the *real* exchange rate $[(1.65/1.28)/1.133=1.46]$.

Between 1985 and 1997, the movement reversed. In 1997, the real dollar exchange rate was 5 percent lower than in 1978.

The bottom chart shows an average of real exchange rates for the countries with which the United States trades. (The average is calculated by weighting each currency by the volume of trade of each country with the United States.) Between 1978 and 1985, this average rose by 57 percent. Between 1985 and 1997, it fell by 28 percent, to a level 13 percent higher than in 1978.

YEN PER DOLLAR, 1978–1998

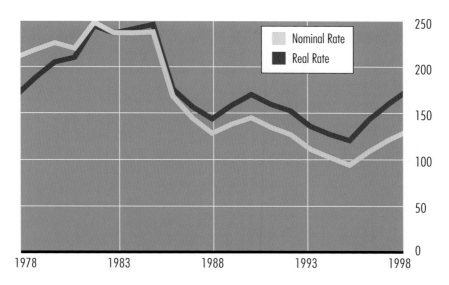

Nominal Rate
Real Rate

REAL VALUE OF THE DOLLAR RELATIVE TO FOREIGN CURRENCIES, 1978–1998

INDEX: 1973=100

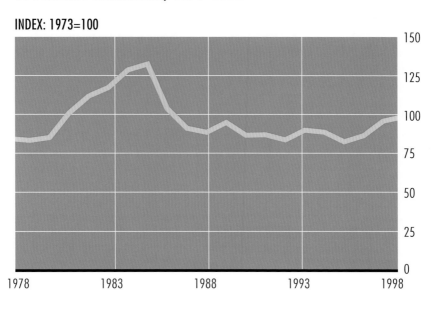

Assets owned by Americans abroad have increased greatly, and assets owned by foreigners in the United States have increased even more.

The increase in the world's wealth plus improvements in financial institutions and the availability of information have contributed to an increase in the flow of capital across national borders. In 1987, wealth owned by Americans abroad equaled about 11 percent of the total wealth in the United States; by 1997, the amount had increased to about 17 percent. Because the United States was a net importer of capital during the period, U.S. assets owned by foreigners rose more, from about 11 percent to 22 percent of U.S. assets.

In the early 1980s, the realization of the increase in foreign ownership of U.S. assets caused much concern, especially when foreigners acquired national symbols such as Radio City Music Hall. But as time passed, this concern dissipated. Foreigners could not take Radio City home with them. They might decide to sell their U.S. assets for dollars and sell the dollars for their home currencies. That transaction would reduce the exchange rate of the dollar. But the possibility was not linked to the foreign ownership of U.S. assets. If Americans decided to sell dollars for yen or deutsche marks, the same result would follow. As the international flow of capital becomes more routine, it becomes more like the domestic flow of capital. Americans investing in Japan come to have the same motivation, information, and behavior as Japanese investing in Japan; the nationality of the suppliers of capital loses its relevance.

Toward the end of the 1990s, concern began to run in the other direction: not about foreign investment here, but about U.S. investment abroad. U.S. investors incurred losses on investments in Asia, Russia, and South America. But there are losses on some domestic investments also, in some industries and at some times. While recent experience has warned of a need for caution, the international movement of capital has been, on the whole, undoubtedly a great benefit to both the suppliers and the recipients of funds.

U.S. ASSETS AND FOREIGN OWNERSHIP, 1987–1997

TRILLIONS OF DOLLARS

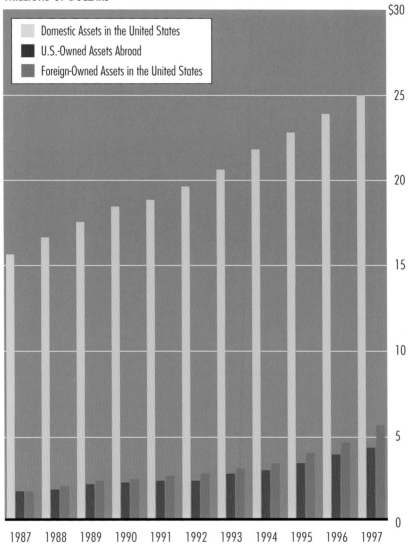

Legend:
- Domestic Assets in the United States
- U.S.-Owned Assets Abroad
- Foreign-Owned Assets in the United States

A Note on the Gross Domestic Product in Constant Prices

This edition of *The Illustrated Guide* takes account of some important changes in the way real GDP, or GDP in constant dollars, is now being calculated and presented by the Bureau of Economic Analysis of the Department of Commerce.

Real GDP is a quantity measure that combines various products and services to derive an overall total. BEA has typically derived quantity measures in constant dollars by dividing figures for sales or receipts in current dollars by price indexes from the Bureau of Labor Statistics. Such calculation has been carried out at the most detailed level allowed by available sales and price data. Detailed figures are then combined to obtain a variety of subtotals, such as real personal consumption expenditures or real private investment, and the subtotals are combined to yield a total real GDP. The gross domestic product and all its breakdowns are expressed in terms of the prices of a given year. In the second edition of *The Illustrated Guide*, for example, real GDP and its breakdowns are shown in terms of 1987 prices for time series that usually go back to 1929. For each of the years, real GDP reflected the quantities produced or sold in that year expressed in 1987 prices.

Problems arise when quantities of various products and services are combined or aggregated in the manner described above. Aggregations that reflect the use of fixed price weights are potentially biased and yield biased results when relative prices change. All prices do not change in the same proportion: some prices may rise rapidly over time, some may rise slowly, and others may decline. The important point is that consumers and businesses alter their buying patterns in response to changes in relative prices. They tend to shift their purchases in favor of items whose prices may have declined or risen least. The further one departs from a price base, the greater the potential bias in a measure such as real GDP obtained through aggregating with fixed price weights.

This means that price weights for combining quantities of different goods and services must be changed. At one time, BEA did this kind of revising every five years. That turned out to be unsatisfactory because while most prices were rising, computer prices were falling rapidly and computer sales were rising. Especially because of computers, the change in real GDP was perceptibly affected, depending on whether all goods and services, and especially computers, were measured in prices prevailing two or three years earlier or in prices, say, five years earlier. After several years of experimentation, BEA decided—beginning in 1996—to use for deflation the so-called chain index, in which price weights for detailed quantity indexes are changed every calendar quarter or year.

One of the consequences of using the kind of chain index employed by BEA is that components of real GDP may not add up to total GDP, and subcomponents may not add up to components. The lack of "additivity" may become serious as one moves away in time from a base period.

Because of the lack of "additivity," BEA has added a "residual" line to most of its tables expressed in constant dollars. When added to the other main components of a table, the residual brings their sum into balance with the real GDP total.

Data and charts based on current dollar figures are not affected, but several charts and their accompanying texts in this volume that are measured in constant dollars have been affected by the foregoing, especially when long periods are involved. Charts showing percentage breakdowns of GDP or breakdowns of a major component such as personal consumption expenditures have been influenced. To minimize computational difficulties, we adopted several practical procedures.

When a residual has been a very small percentage of a total, it has been ignored. To avoid large residuals, we sometimes reduced the number of years illustrated in a chart. On some occasions, it has been preferable to take a midpoint of a long span of years in selecting a base period for a price index. When the residuals have been very large, we have given up showing a percentage breakdown of real GDP. Sometimes it has been possible to demonstrate an underlying point regarding a long period simply by showing quantity data in chain index form.

For further information, see J. Steven Landefeld and Robert P. Parker, "BEA's Chain Indexes, Time Series, and Measures of Long-Term Economic Growth," *Survey of Current Business*, volume 77, number 5, May 1997.

Some important statistical issues that are touched on here are taken up in part fifteen, "Price Indexes and the Quality of Life."

Sources

Part	Page	Source	Part	Page	Source	Part	Page	Source
Part One	5	I, J, U	Part Seven	105	I, N, JJ		201	N
	7	CC		107	I, N, JJ		203	N
	9	J, X, CC		109	N, JJ		205	E, N
	11	J, II		111	J, N, JJ	Part Thirteen	209	I, J
	13	I, J, V	Part Eight	115	J		211	BB
Part Two	17	I		117	J		215	BB
	19	I		119	J		217	I
	21	I		213	I		219	BB
	23	I, JJ		121	J		221	W
Part Three	27	I		123	J		223	I
	29	I		125	J, GG		225	BB
	31	I		127	J		227	O
	33	I		129	D		229	CC
Part Four	37	I		131	I		231	BB
	39	I		133	I		233	BB
	41	I	Part Nine	137	B, C, U, X, EE		235	H
	43	I		139	J, EE		237	BB
	45	E, I		141	C	Part Fourteen	241	L
	47	I		143	J		243	I
	49	I		145	J		245	L
	51	I		147	Z		247	H
Part Five	55	N	Part Ten	151	J, FF		249	J
	57	J, N, JJ		153	E, J	Part Fifteen	253	A
	59	N		155	S		255	N
	61	I		157	I		257	I
	63	I		159	J, JJ		259	K
	65	N		161	I		261	I, R
	67	I		163	N		263	Q
	69	N	Part Eleven	167	P	Part Sixteen	267	I
	71	I		169	I, E, JJ		269	I
	73	I		171	E		271	I
	75	I		173	E		273	HH
	77	CC		175	I, E, JJ		275	I
	79	N		177	E		277	E, N
	81	N		179	E		279	I
Part Six	85	N	Part Twelve	183	G			
	87	N		185	I, AA			
	89	I		187	N, AA			
	91	N		189	T			
	93	N		191	N			
	95	I		193	N			
	97	M, N, JJ		195	N			
	99	N		197	N			
	101	F		199	H, N			

References

A.   Advisory Commission to Study the Consumer Price Index, *Final Report of the Advisory Commission to Study the Consumer Price Index* (Washington, D.C.: Government Printing Office, 1996). This is known as the Boskin report.

B.   Betson, David M., and Jennifer L. Warlick, "Alternative Historical Trends in Poverty," *American Economic Review*, vol. 88, no. 2, May 1998.

C.   Blackburn, McKinley, *Comparing Poverty* (Washington, D.C.: AEI Press, 1997).

D.   Blau, Francine, "Trends in the Well-Being of American Women," *Journal of Economic Literature*, vol. 36, no. 1, March 1998.

E.   Board of Governors of the Federal Reserve System.

F.   Board of Trustees, Federal Old-Age and Survivors Insurance and Disability Insurance Trust Funds, *1998 Annual Report of the Board of Trustees, Federal Old-Age and Survivors Insurance and Disability Insurance Trust Funds* (Washington, D.C.: Government Printing Office, 1998).

G.   Conference Board.

H.   Congressional Budget Office.

I.   Department of Commerce, Bureau of Economic Analysis.

J.   Department of Commerce, Bureau of the Census.

K.   Department of Energy, Energy Information Administration.

L.   Department of Health and Human Services, Health Care Financing Administration.

M.   Department of Health and Human Services, National Center for Health Statistics.

N.   Department of Labor, Bureau of Labor Statistics.

O.   Department of the Treasury, Office of Tax Analysis.

P.   Dow Jones and Co., Inc.

Q.   Eisner, Robert, *The Total Incomes System of Accounts* (Chicago: University of Chicago Press, 1989).

R.   Environmental Protection Agency.

S.   Federal Communications Commission, Common Carrier Bureau's Industry Analysis Division.

T.   Friedman, Milton, and Anna J. Schwartz, *Monetary Trends in the United States and United Kingdom* (Chicago: University of Chicago Press, 1982).

U.   Jorgenson, Dale W., "Did We Lose the War on Poverty?" *Journal of Economic Perspectives*, vol. 12, no. 1, winter 1998.

V.   Kendrick, John, *Productivity Trends in the United States* (New York: Arno Press, 1975).

W.   Kollman, Geoffrey, "Social Security: The Relationship of Taxes and Benefits for Past, Present, and Future Retirees," Washington, D.C., Congressional Research Service, 1998.

X.   Ladd, Everett Carll, and Karlyn H. Bowman, *Attitudes toward Economic Inequality* (Washington, D.C.: AEI Press, 1998).

Y.   Maddison, Angus, *Monitoring the World Economy*, 1820–1992 (Paris: Development Center for the Organization for Economic Cooperation and Development, 1995).

Z.   Mincey, Ronald B., and Susan J. Wiener, "The Underclass in the 1980s: Changing Concept, Constant Reality," Washington, D.C., Urban Institute, 1993.

AA. Moore, Geoffrey H., ed., *Business Cycle Indicators, Basic Data on Cyclical Indicators*, vol. 2 (Princeton: Princeton University Press, 1961).

BB. Office of Management and Budget.

CC. Organization for Economic Cooperation and Development.

DD. Slesnick, Daniel T., "Consumption, Needs, and Inequality," *International Economic Review*, vol. 35, August 1994.

EE. Slesnick, Daniel T., "Gaining Ground: Poverty in the Postwar United States," *Journal of Political Economy*, vol. 101, no. 1, 1993.

FF. Small Business Administration.

GG. Smith, J. P., and F. R. Welch, "Black Economic Progress after Myrdal," *Journal of Economic Literature*, June 1989, and calculations of J. P. Smith.

HH. Whichard, Obie G., and Jeffrey H. Lowe, "The Statistics Corner: An Ownership-Based Supplement to the U.S. Balance of Payments Accounts," *Business Economics*, vol. 33, no. 2, April 1998.

II. World Bank.

JJ. Authors' calculations.

About the Authors

Herbert Stein had been for many years a senior fellow at the American Enterprise Institute at the time of his death in September 1999. He served as a member of the Council of Economic Advisers from 1969 to 1971 and as the chairman from 1972 to 1974. He was also a member of President Reagan's Economic Policy Advisory Board and a consultant to the State Department on the economy of Israel. Mr. Stein was the A. Willis Robertson Professor of Economics Emeritus at the University of Virginia, a member of the board of contributors of the *Wall Street Journal*, a monthly contributor to *Slate*, and the recipient in 1989 of the Frank E. Seidman Award in Political Economy.

Mr. Stein's books include *What I Think: Essays on Economics, Politics, and Life* (AEI, 1998); *On the Other Hand: Essays on Economics, Economists, and Politics* (AEI, 1995); *Presidential Economics: The Making of Economic Policy from Roosevelt to Clinton* (AEI, rev. ed. 1994); *The Fiscal Revolution in America: Policy in Pursuit of Reality* (AEI, 2d rev. ed. 1996); and *Washington Bedtime Stories* (Free Press, 1986).

Murray Foss is a visiting scholar at the American Enterprise Institute. He was a senior research associate at the National Bureau of Economic Research from 1975 to 1978 and a senior staff economist in charge of forecasting at the Council of Economic Advisers from 1970 to 1975. He was the editor of the Survey of Current Business and the chief of the Current Business Analysis Division of the Bureau of Economic Analysis of the Department of Commerce

Mr. Foss is the author of *Shiftwork, Capital Hours and Productivity Change* (Kluwer, 1997); *Changes in the Workweek of Fixed Capital: U.S. Manufacturing, 1929–1976* (AEI, 1981); and *Changing Utilization of Fixed Capital: An Element in Long-Term Growth* (AEI, 1984). He edited the NBER conference volume *The U.S. National Income and Product Accounts* (University of Chicago Press, 1983), and was the coeditor of the NBER conference volume *Price Measurements and Their Uses* (University of Chicago Press, 1993).

A Note on the Book

This book was edited by Ann Petty of the AEI Press. Kenneth Krattenmaker and Jean-Marie Navetta, both of the AEI Press, designed the book and drew the charts. The text was set in Garamond and Futura. Jean-Marie Navetta set the type. Fontana Lithograph, Inc., of Cheverly, Maryland, printed and bound the book, using permanent acid-free paper.

The AEI Press is the publisher for the American Enterprise Institute for Public Policy Research, 1150 17th Street, N.W., Washington, D.C. 20036: Christopher DeMuth, publisher; James Morris, director; Ann Petty, editor; Leigh Tripoli, editor; Cheryl Weissman, editor; Kenneth Krattenmaker, art director and production manager; and Jean-Marie Navetta, production assistant.